T0326054

the day I met

BRIAN CLOUGH

...And Other Tributes

Includes memories from Brian Clough's family, friends and fans

the day I met
BRIAN CLOUGH
...And Other Tributes

Includes memories from Brian Clough's family, friends and fans

Compiled by Marcus Alton

Editor of brianclough.com

First published in Great Britain in 2011 by The Derby Books Publishing Company
Limited, Derby, DE21 4SZ.

This paperback edition published in Great Britain in 2013 by DB Publishing,
an imprint of JMD Media Ltd

ISBN 978-1-908234-98-8

Printed and bound in the UK by Copytech (UK) Ltd Peterborough

Author's royalties to the Brian Clough Memorial Fund

Dedicated to Sarah, always my inspiration, and my
wonderful Mum and Dad

INTRODUCTION

By Marcus Alton

Meeting Brian Clough was usually an unforgettable experience. Whether it was for 30 seconds or 30 minutes, simply being in his company was guaranteed to create memories which would last a lifetime. The Clough magic would cast a spell to excite, entertain and leave you guessing about what he was going to do next. And it was that unpredictability which kept players, fans and the media on their toes.

Just ask the man whose car broke down on the A52 (now Brian Clough Way) during a storm. The last thing he expected was a knock on his window and the offer of help – from yes, you guessed it. Or the young lad who was often in trouble with the Police but found his life transformed after he had a kick-about with Cloughie in a park.

Then there was the hospital radio reporter who beat the national press pack to secure a 15-minute interview with the great man; the paramedic who was left almost speechless when the Master Manager stopped to thank him for the vital work he was doing –

and the young boy who was told he couldn't leave the dinner table until he'd eaten all his tomatoes.

Never to be considered a shrinking violet, Brian once spotted one of England's greatest-ever strikers at an airport and proceeded to kiss him on the cheek before simply walking off. But not all the surprises were conjured up by Clough. Sometimes he was on the receiving end. One of his former players described to me how he poured a bucket of water over his boss – by accident. You can probably guess the result. These are just some of the many memories contained in this book.

There's no doubt Brian Clough had a profound effect on many, many people. He once told a BBC local radio phone-in about how he'd visited a hospital in Derby to see a man who had only a few weeks to live. The patient had told his wife that one of his last remaining wishes was to meet you-know-who. So Brian went along to see him and they chatted for sometime – the man communicating with help from his wife because of the effect of his illness. Brian recalled: 'He told me there was just one thing that really upset him that year. I thought he was going to say it was all to do with me retiring from football. But no. He told me, "I realised I've just got my season ticket and I can't use it up!"' It was the type of one-liner that Brian himself would have been proud of. I have no doubt that Cloughie's visit that day meant so much to that man and his wife.

Cloughie's influence around the world can never be underestimated. I have even been contacted recently by a young fan in Bangalore in India. Despite being born only two years before Brian retired, this young man explained that, although he lived thousands of miles away, his life has been profoundly affected by watching archive footage and learning more about the Master Manager.

Over the years, since setting-up the non-profit-making tribute website, I have collected so many tributes and anecdotes about Brian Clough. Some have come from fans who wanted to share their memories of meeting their hero. Others are from former colleagues, players and journalists. So I decided it would be fitting to put them all into one volume for posterity. And more than that – I am very proud to include memories from Brian's widow, Barbara, and their daughter Elizabeth, as well as Brian's eldest brother Joe and sister Doreen.

When my tribute website celebrated its 10th anniversary, Mrs Clough kindly sent a message of congratulations. 'Although Brian was not really from the computer generation, I am sure the website would have made him smile,' she said. 'He certainly thought it was tremendous to receive all the e-mails from fans which were forwarded to him.'

Mrs Clough said it was wonderful to know that fans from all over the world still send their tributes and messages by e-mail. She said she hoped the website would continue for many years to come. 'It is very comforting to know that Brian is still thought of so fondly by so many people.' Mrs Clough's message can be read in full on the website.

I am particularly grateful to the Clough family for their support of this book, which has been a labour of love for me. Having got to know them through running the tribute website, launching the knighthood campaign and then setting-up the fund-raising committee for a statue in Nottingham, it has been a real privilege to meet them and share their memories.

I was fortunate to meet Brian a number of times, both as a journalist and as a fan. I'm pleased to say I was never disappointed. In fact, those meetings led to memories I will treasure forever.

Here are some of my top encounters with Cloughie (in no particular order)...

My first radio interview with Cloughie.

I was working for the BBC in London when I received a phone call one Tuesday afternoon. 'How d'you fancy interviewing Brian Clough on Saturday morning?' It was a colleague of mine in the East Midlands, with an offer I couldn't refuse. Cloughie had rarely conducted any radio interviews since his retirement 18 months earlier, so this was a fantastic opportunity.

My colleague – who knew I was a huge fan of Brian – explained that Cloughie was planning to do a signing session for his new autobiography and would be available for an interview at a book shop. Without hesitation, I said I would arrange to return from London in order to do the interview for local radio on Saturday. Then came the knock-out punch. 'Oh, by the way, the interview will be live.'

The prospect of interviewing Brian Clough for the first time was incredible. But the thought of doing that live – with no chance of editing it if things went wrong – made it even more nerve-wracking. Meeting my hero was one thing, but speaking to him with thousands of people listening was quite another. Would he try to catch me out with one of his famous one-liners? Would I be lost for words and forget what to ask him? Would he arrive on time

– or be running late and we would miss the live slot on the radio programme? And what about the broadcasting equipment – would it operate in the shop and not cut-out at the last minute? All these questions – and much more – were whirring around my head as the morning of the interview finally arrived.

I walked to the shop, carrying the sound equipment over my shoulder, and got there in plenty of time. The staff at the shop showed me into a room at the back and I quickly tested the magical box of broadcasting equipment which would hopefully transmit my live interview. That was the first hurdle successfully negotiated. Now came the big challenge. I could hear his voice as he arrived in the shop.

A few moments later, he made his way into the room where I was waiting. He was discussing something with one of the assistants and I got the impression that not everything had gone smoothly that morning. I hoped it wasn't a sign of things to come. He turned towards me and we were introduced. 'Hello Mr Clough, it's great to see you,' are the few words I can remember saying, before I explained it would be a live interview and we would be on the air within a matter of minutes. I contacted the studio and said we were ready to start. But my heart was racing even faster when I was told there would be a short delay, until the presenter was able to introduce me. 'Shall I go and start signing some of the books?' asked Brian, turning to the assistant. 'No, please, Mr Clough – it'll only be a few minutes and then we're live on the air,' I explained. The last thing I wanted was for the star guest to walk out of that room and my interview opportunity to be lost once the crowds of fans arrived.

It was time to take charge of the situation. 'You've got to cross to me now, Mr Clough is waiting,' I snapped down the microphone, making it quite clear to the studio that it was now or never. The presenter faded down whatever record he was playing and explained that his reporter was about to speak to a football legend. I was on.

The interview began with me referring to the weather (it was pouring with rain) before I asked Mr Clough how a life of leisure was suiting him since retirement. 'Absolutely magnificently,' came the reply. 'I'm enjoying every second. I think I should have done it five years ago.'

He said it was a wonderful feeling to get up each morning knowing that he could simply do whatever he fancied doing. 'I've got my grandchildren, I've got holidays, I've got a garden, I've got lanes to walk down, I've got your lovely smiling face to look at on a Saturday – God forbid!'

And that was it – with that wonderful one-liner at the end of his answer, he'd broken the ice and I knew he was in the mood for an entertaining interview.

He was particularly outspoken about one of his favourite subjects – the job security (or lack of it) of football managers. There had been a spate of managerial sackings, and I asked him what he thought about the situation.

'It's been a mad month for top-class managers and top-class clubs,' he said. 'I don't know what's going on in the minds of chairmen and directors at the moment, but they're not coming up with remedies, they're just a short-term answer and it's reached epidemic proportions.

'If they really want to show they're sincere, then by all means sack the managers – but they should resign as chairmen too, because initially it's their decision to appoint them.'

He told me that the fear of getting the sack should be removed from the thoughts of managers altogether. 'The game's hard enough without having this in the background every time you get out of bed each morning.'

And I'm sure there are plenty of managers out there who feel those views remain as valid today as they did when Brian expressed them so passionately back in 1994.

He got out of his chair and kissed me on the cheek.

I will never forget the moment when Brian gave me a big hug and a kiss! It happened after I asked him to sign a precious photograph. I'd read in a local newspaper that he was going to be the special guest at a fête in Derbyshire, where I was working at the time.

Although he'd retired from football management, he was still keen to help the local community by appearing at a fund-raising event. So I went along and took the photo I hoped he would sign. It was a large and unusual picture of Cloughie in the dressing room with his victorious Nottingham Forest team after they had just secured their place in the 1991 FA Cup Final.

The photo was a great memory of a sunny day at Villa Park when I watched Forest beat West Ham in the semi-final. The Great Man didn't often invite the media into his dressing room, but on this occasion he had. The photographer captured a classic scene, with Cloughie sitting in his dressing gown alongside his players and backroom staff. I was determined to get everyone on the photo to sign it.

I spent several weeks waiting outside the Forest dressing room after training sessions, in the hope of getting the various players to add their names. And they all did. Names like Roy Keane, Stuart

Pearce, Des Walker, Brian Laws and Cloughie's son, Nigel, who is pictured with a towel round his waist. The backroom staff signed it too, but the one signature which remained missing was that of Cloughie himself.

So that morning I headed for the local féte, carrying the photo in a large brown padded envelope. It was a fairly low-key event and there was a small number of people waiting with me for Cloughie's autograph. He was sitting behind a small table, signing everything that was presented to him, from books to scraps of paper. He took time to speak to everyone as we queued.

Then it was my turn. I carefully pulled the photo out of the envelope, wondering what his reaction would be when he saw it. His eyes lit-up as he gazed across that dressing room scene, as if the memories were flooding back. Looking more closely, he could see all his players had signed it.

'I wondered if you could sign this for me please, Mr Clough. Yours is the only signature I'm missing,' I said, my hands trembling as I handed him the pen. 'My pleasure, young man,' came the reply, as he carefully started to add his signature.

Handing back the pen, he took one more look at the photo. 'Happy days,' he said, nodding. 'Thanks Mr Clough, you've made my day,' I said, even though my mouth was dry with nerves. At that point, he looked up at me and got out of his chair. 'Young man, you've made my day too,' he said and stepped towards me. He opened his arms and gave me a huge bear hug and a kiss on the cheek.

Looking back, I'm glad that photo brought back some good memories for him that day. It will always do the same for me too.

It felt like being caught in the Cloughie headlights.

I've got to admit that I felt like a startled rabbit – caught directly in the firing line – when Cloughie picked me out during a signing session for one of his books. I feared I was about to receive an ear-bashing! It followed a visit I'd made to his house to deliver some get well messages. I'd received the e-mails from fans around the world who wanted to send their best wishes for his recovery from a liver transplant. I handed them over to Mrs Clough who had answered the door to a very nervous visitor.

A few months later, he was the star attraction as he signed copies of the updated edition of his autobiography at WH Smith in Nottingham's Victoria Centre. The queue of admirers eager to meet him spilled out of the main entrance of the store. As Cloughie sat at a table signing books and other memorabilia, I was standing a few feet away, taking photos for the website.

Suddenly, he stopped signing the books for the long queue of fans and looked-up in my direction. Wagging that famous finger, he pointed towards me and, slightly raising his voice, asked: 'Are you the young man who brought that pile of messages for me?' I became frozen to the spot, like a frightened rabbit caught in the headlights of a car. Was I about to get a rollicking for turning-up at his house unannounced? It was obvious he had recognised me, so honesty seemed the best policy. 'Yes, Mr Clough, it was me,' I replied.

He then got out of his chair, leant forward and put his arm out to shake my hand. 'Thanks very much for all those messages you delivered, young man,' he said. 'It was very much appreciated.'

He then suggested we should have a chat – which we did when the signing session was over. It was wonderful to spend 15 minutes in his company, during which he told me how well he was feeling – it had obviously given him a boost to receive the messages of support. He was also impressed with the turn-out that day. 'To see so many people has been nothing short of incredible,' he told me. I also took the opportunity to record an interview for BBC radio...

He told me my appearance made him seem good-looking – and I was flattered!

More than eight years after my first interview with Brian, I had the chance to speak to him again for the BBC – thankfully this time the interview was recorded (a real bonus, for which I breathed a sigh of relief half-way through the conversation!). I told him he was looking well. 'Young man, thank you. I'm in good nick,' he said. I asked him how important the support of his wife Barbara had been. 'It's been incredible,' he replied – and with tongue firmly in cheek he added: 'I thought about changing her for a younger model a few years ago, but she's stuck it for 44 years, so it's been fine.'

He described how Barbara had taken the phone call one Sunday night to tell them that a liver was available for the transplant and it was on its way from Ireland. They then made the trip to the hospital in the North East. 'We got to Newcastle in two and a half hours because my daughter drove me up there and she drives too fast – all women do, actually. But it's just co-incidental she's a good driver and we got there.'

I asked him if he could remember his first request for something to eat after the operation. I knew it was a question which promised a humorous answer. But I didn't quite expect just how comical he would be – and, at that point, I was incredibly grateful it was a recorded interview.

He told me he had asked the hospital staff for an apple sandwich. 'I quite like apple sandwiches – the only thing is, they don't keep apples in hospitals.' I then started to wonder where this answer was going. He described how the nurse was short-sighted and he feared he might lose certain parts of his anatomy. 'It's not live, is it?' asked Cloughie, looking at the microphone I was holding. 'Thankfully not,' I replied, just about keeping my laughter in check. 'Ah, that's alright. You won't last another six months in this job if you follow me around.'

But the great quotes didn't end there. While describing his surgeon, Derek Manas, as 'incredible', he dished-out the type of praise which could only come from Old Big 'Ead. 'He's supposed to be in the top three in the country, but he told me he was the best. Conceited – it's incredible. I said to him, "They'll have to widen the hospital doors if you and I walk in together, because they'd never get both heads through one door, would they?"'

I'm proud to say that I, too, didn't escape being on the receiving end of a classic one-liner. As he praised the whole NHS team at Newcastle's Freeman Hospital, he added: 'I thanked them then –

and I'm thanking them again now. It's an incredible situation and an incredible experience. But I'm in good nick. I want to take you around with me for the next three, four or five weeks, because you definitely make me better looking than I am – and it's understandable obviously!'

That bottle of bubbly – he told me: 'It goes well in the bath.'
When I got out of bed at some unearthly hour one Saturday morning in 2002, the last thing I expected was to receive a bottle of champagne from Brian Clough a few hours later. Admittedly, my alarm clock had been set for an early-morning wake-up call in the hope of meeting my hero. But little did I think it would turn into such a special day.

Cloughie was due to sign copies of his book *Walking on Water* at a supermarket in Nottingham. It was 17 August and the very first signing session he did for the book – in fact, the official publication date was several days later. The publishers had said in advance that he would sign copies for the first 300 people who turned up.

I was so determined to meet my football hero, and have a few signed copies of the book, that I arrived at Asda in West Bridgford more than five hours before he was due to appear. And I was not alone. My girlfriend (now wife) Sarah was with me too. Luckily for me, Sarah is almost as big a fan of Cloughie as I am. So, there we were, standing outside Asda at quarter to six in the morning. Some would say that's dedication. Others might say it was pure madness. But whatever you think, I'll always be glad we did it.

When the doors opened at six-o-clock and there were still no other fans around, it began to dawn on us that we would be the first in the queue to meet Cloughie that morning. The nerves began to jangle a little as we anticipated coming face-to-face with the world's most charismatic football manager. What would he say to us? Would he tell us we were completely crackers for waiting so long and send us away with a clip round the ear? Or would he treat us like long-lost friends who'd been waiting patiently for that special moment?

Gradually the queue had grown behind us during the morning, until it snaked out of the main entrance and into the sunshine. The supermarket staff looked after us well and soon we were on first-name terms with them. They even made sure we had something to eat and drink.

When the man himself finally appeared from a side-door, there was spontaneous applause and the crowd sang his name. For a moment he stood still with a big grin on his face and soaked-up the adulation. He blew a kiss and shouted above the singing, 'Good morning to you!'

The outpouring of affection and respect from hundreds of people was quite overwhelming – and was recorded for posterity by a TV camera crew. It still sends shivers down my spine when I watch it back now. And at the head of the queue, Sarah and I were both shaking with nerves as we prepared to meet the legend. 'Where's Sarah? I've been told I've got to meet Sarah,' said Cloughie as he started to make his way through the crowd. An assistant from the publishing company realised it was going to be a difficult task for Brian to get through the mass of people and she guided him towards us.

He approached us with a big smile, shook Sarah's hand and then mine. 'It's great to meet you, Mr Clough,' I said. 'Nice to meet you, too, young man,' he replied, before asking where we lived. When Sarah said she came from Gedling, his eyes lit-up. 'That's a pit area, isn't it? I've got a statue from Gedling Pit. They gave it to me.' His support of the miners during the 1984 strike will live long in the memory of many people, and it once again brought back memories for him as he chatted to us.

Cloughie then presented us with a bottle of champagne for being the first in the queue. It was a bottle of Moet and Chandon – the significance of which was not lost on the Great Man himself. In the books he was signing that day, he admitted that drink had had an adverse affect on his health and there were times it had impaired his judgement. So, as he handed-over the bottle of bubbly, he joked, 'You're trying to get me on the booze again, aren't you?' The crowd laughed as they watched the Great Man, who was in fine form. A newspaper photographer, who knew Cloughie well, asked us to pose for a photo. Trevor Bartlett from the *Nottingham Evening Post* had worked with the Master Manager for many years, and he captured some great pictures that day. As the three of us stood close together, Cloughie looked at me, smiled and joked to Trevor, 'Hurry up, I've heard he's famous for getting people's wallets.' There was more laughter.

Then Brian gave Sarah a kiss. It was a special moment and one I know Sarah will never forget. In fact, he kissed her on the cheek twice – to ensure Trevor got the photo. 'Thank you, Mr Clough' she said, being careful not to drop the champagne. Cloughie pointed to the bubbly. 'It goes well in the bath,' he told us. 'We used to bathe in that. It's easy when you win to have a glass of champagne. And the excuse when I lost was I thought I'd drown my bloomin' sorrows.'

'But that didn't happen very often – you didn't lose many, Mr Clough,' said Sarah, as Cloughie sat down to start signing our books. 'That's right,' he replied. 'I had a good run, pet, I had a good run.' And what an understatement that was. He was never known for his modesty, and it seemed incredible for Brian Clough to describe his all-conquering, trophy-winning seasons as 'a good run.' I am sure many managers in the modern game would give anything for the same 'good run' that the Master Manager enjoyed.

Despite the long queue, Cloughie lavished his time on us that morning and signed everything we wanted. He even took time to talk about his family. 'I've got five grandchildren, two of them boys – and they run me ragged.' He told us how he took them to see matches at Burton Albion, where his son Nigel was then manager. 'It costs me a fortune at half-time for my grandchildren, with all the chips and burgers,' he told us. 'You'd think they never got fed at home!'

We left that morning absolutely elated about meeting our hero – and I know it was a feeling shared by many more of his fans, of all ages, who treasured their few moments meeting the Great Man.

The following collection of memories and tributes is just a small indication of the effect Brian Clough had on so many people – how he touched the lives of countless fans around the world. The book is the result of the many e-mails I've received over the years and the conversations I've had with his family, friends and fans. One former player, who won the European Cup under Cloughie, described to me his shock when he heard Brian had passed away. But he summed things up beautifully when he added: 'I feel sorry for anyone who never had the chance to meet him. Whether you liked the way he said things or not, you were always a better person for having met him.'

Barbara Clough, Brian's wife: 'He knew instinctively what to say and when a special word was needed.'

First of all, I want to say that it is a pleasure to add my voice to those others recalling meetings and memories of Brian.

It is well-documented that Brian and I met in Rea's Cafe which was really a 'coffee-bar' popular in the Fifties with teenagers and which was owned and run by singer Chris Rea's Dad and uncle. I knew who Brian was, of course, because my Dad never missed a game at Ayresome Park so I knew that Brian, to my Dad's great delight, was scoring goal after goal for his beloved Boro.

I had no way of knowing what a wonderfully varied life we would have – a roller-coaster rather than a sedate, predictable carousel. A quote from a film and one with which many working in professional football will identify.

I know many people will expect me to reminisce about football and the marvellous European Cups etc., but I want to say that the main memory I have of Brian is of his overwhelming generosity. This included the time he gave to the people he met and is one of the reasons so many people from all walks of life paid tribute to him. Like his actions in football, he knew instinctively what to say and when a special word was needed.

His friends and family, but especially his family, benefited most from this generosity of spirit. I spoke of this and how many of them are leading much nicer lives because of him in a recent TV documentary. Sadly, what I said wasn't included, and I so wish it had been.

As I said, I think most people will have expected me to recall the heady days of the wonderfully entertaining football and, of course, the unforgettable trips to Munich, Madrid and Wembley. I will never ever forget these but, side by side with all the quirky stories and anecdotes about Brian, it is this kindness and generosity I remember most.

Elizabeth Clough, Brian's daughter: 'I honestly didn't consider it too unusual when he stopped the car on the way to school to give other kids a lift.'

I don't need to dig deep for memories of my Dad, I'm surrounded by them and, as anyone who has lost a loved parent will agree, the longer they are gone and the older you yourself become, the more precious the memories.

To use a cliché, but a true one, to me my Dad was just my Dad. Of course as I grew up I realised his job was different from those of other kids' Dads and that he was well known, but I honestly didn't consider it too unusual when he stopped the car on the way to school to give other kids a lift (not always a popular one with me, I've got to admit) or that there was anything unusual about inviting a couple of little lads from the North East that he met outside Newcastle FC's ground to share our family home for a period of time. Actually, one of them recently wrote to my Mum, thanking her and telling her he would never forget what my Dad had done for him.

I couldn't understand why, at parties, people didn't get the words right to *New York, New York* and *That's Life*, but then they obviously hadn't spent 20 years travelling in my Dad's car! I still know every syllable and intonation of *Leroy Brown*, and I love that I do.

My Dad worked extremely hard all his life and was exceptionally generous – that's what I meant when I said I'm surrounded by memories. I'm aware every single day of his immense kindness, the homes he helped provide that people still live in, the employment he found and businesses he supplied that people still work in, places they have visited as a direct result of his generosity, not to mention the entertainment and pleasure he gave and still gives to an awful lot of football fans. He always wanted as many people as possible to benefit from his position – a true socialist in every sense of the word.

He had a reputation for, shall we say, talking a lot, well I never heard him or my Mum speak about any of these things. The only other occasions I remember him being a wee bit muted were when family, or those he considered friends, consciously let him down. He couldn't understand it and neither can I, but insecurity and envy can lead individuals from all walks of life to behave badly.

How can I not mention the glorious football trips to Wembley and to Europe – such happy, exciting times. Those who were fortunate enough to be there will never forget and although I was too young to remember the success at Derby, the hundreds, probably thousands, of tributes left by both sets of supporters and from all over the world – and the 15,000 who attended his Memorial Service – more than confirm the legacy left by my Dad.

I am proud, I miss him, and in answer to his request that he hoped people would say he contributed, yes Dad, you did, more than most.

Joe Clough, Brian Clough's eldest brother: 'Brian had a special role at my wedding reception.'

When we were younger, I remember playing in the same football team as Brian – it was for the Great Broughton side which played in a local league on Saturday afternoons. We had to get changed in the Temperance Hall. I played half-back and he was the centre-forward. We did well – in fact, the team was unbeaten and won the league. You could see how skilful Brian was as a footballer even then.

Brian liked to be in charge, even when he was a lad. When I married my wife June in 1950, Brian was about 15 years old and at the wedding reception he was in charge of the children's table. The food was still rationed in those days and we had spam, salad and cakes. Brian organised all the kids – he told each one which cake they could have. He was very good at telling them what to do. You could tell who was the boss even in those days!

On one occasion, I remember returning home on leave from the Navy to hear that one of my brothers had been involved in a tussle with a lad across the road – probably a few slaps and punches. Our Mam was told it was my brother Billy who'd been involved because this other lad was Billy's age, so she had a go at him about it and promised to give him a clip round the ear. But it was actually Brian who'd been involved – even though he was two years younger and much smaller. But Brian was lucky and managed to get away with it.

When Brian first started seeing Barbara in Middlesbrough, he would call at my house on his way to meeting her and spruce himself up. He'd always make sure his hair looked good. He liked to look smart when he was going out.

As a family, we used to go on regular holidays to Blackpool. It was a highlight of the year. On one holiday there, when Brian was a lad, we took a roll of film for the camera, and he insisted on appearing on every photo. He liked to be the centre of attention even then!

Doreen Elder, Brian Clough's sister: 'We danced to a Frank Sinatra song.'

I've got lots and lots of lovely memories of Brian. He was such a caring and loving brother. He would phone me two or three times a week to see if I was OK and whether I wanted anything. Wherever he was, he would always make sure he phoned us. He would say: 'I can only give you my love, which you've got, and my money, which is yours.'

I used to watch all the Forest home matches, and I'll never forget his last match in charge at the City Ground. He waved to the crowd as they sang his name. Afterwards, I was with our cousins and friends in the room next to his office. Then Archie Gemmill came through and said 'the Gaffer wants you.' So I went through to see Brian and we had a dance to a Frank Sinatra song. It was a very emotional evening and one I'll never forget.

Ron Roberts, Nottingham: 'Mr Clough knocked on my window.'

I'll never forget the day that I came face-to-face with Brian Clough – and he offered me a helping hand. I was driving along the A52 (now the Brian Clough Way) to pick-up my daughter from school. There was torrential rain and the water was running down the road. It was terrible weather and my car just cut-out because of all the water. It came to a complete standstill. To make things worse, I was stuck in the middle lane of the dual carriageway, near Bramcote Baths. As the traffic was starting to queue-up behind me, I heard a knock on my car window. It was Mr Clough. He was wearing a football jacket and tracksuit bottoms. 'Can I help you, young man?' he asked. Without hesitation, and in the pouring rain, he helped to push my car to the side of the road. He asked if I needed a lift, but I said I'd be alright. I couldn't believe I'd just met Brian Clough – and he'd helped to push my car! I'll always remember that day.

Paul Hart, former Nottingham Forest player and manager: 'He said 'Call me Brian' – I never did.'

I can still remember the first time I met Brian Clough. It was three days after the season finished in 1983. Leeds United were in the Second Division, and I got a call from the manager to tell me that a club was interested in signing me – it was Nottingham Forest. I then met the Gaffer after a reserve game at Elland Road – I actually met him in the office of the Leeds United manager. I said 'Hello, Mr Clough.' He said, 'Call me Brian.' Of course, I never did.

He then began to persuade me to join him at Forest. But he said, 'If you think you are going to get the money you are on at Leeds, you're mistaken.' And in the same breath he said, 'I'm not leaving until you agree.' I took a huge cut in wages, but it was the best decision I ever made. He was the best boss I worked for. He kept things simple, and I enjoyed playing for him.

After I left Forest, I suffered a broken leg while playing for Birmingham and had to go into hospital. The Gaffer diverted the Nottingham Forest team bus to Birmingham so that the players could visit me in hospital. That was just typical of the man, it was a fantastic gesture.

Some years later, after I got the sack as Chesterfield manager, the Gaffer tried to get work for me at other clubs. Then I got a call and he told me, 'If you're as good as I'm telling other people, you'd better come to work for me.' I then started working with the young players at Forest. He looked after me, and I'll always be grateful for that.

Terry Bell, one of Cloughie's first signings at Hartlepool: 'The day I poured a bucket of water over Brian Clough.'

It felt really good when I knew that Brian Clough wanted to sign me. Even in those early days at Hartlepool, you could tell that Brian had all the qualities to be a successful manager. He was great to play for and very down to earth. But one day I got into trouble. As players for him at Hartlepool, we were always playing practical jokes on each other. On one occasion I got into the dressing room to find that someone had cut all the toes out of my socks. So I thought I would get my own back on the lad that did it.

I decided to climb up onto the roof of the dressing room with a bucket of water. Some of my teammates would then signal to me when the lad in question was walking past and I would throw the bucket of water over him. So I waited and finally got the signal – but unfortunately it wasn't who I expected! Guess who was walking by? I poured the bucket of water over Brian Clough! To make it even worse, he wasn't wearing his tracksuit – he was going to a funeral that day so he was wearing a suit. And it got absolutely soaked! As a result he fined me a week's wages.

We had some great times at Hartlepool. I remember he used to take us down to the beach for training sessions. Brian had been an outstanding goalscorer, so as a centre-forward who scored a lot of goals I really enjoyed playing for him. I looked up to him. In one match, I was running towards the goalkeeper to get on the end of a cross, but the goalkeeper beat me to it. I ran up to the 'keeper and then turned away, but as he kicked the ball out, it hit me on the head and went into the net. What a way to score a goal! Brian was very pleased with that one.

Ken Smales, former Nottingham Forest club secretary: 'I appreciated his friendship.'

Brian – like most of us – had, what a friend of mine used to call, a selective memory, remembering the things he wanted and unconsciously dismissing those that he thought of no great importance. The players will tell you that he could recall every incident in a game without making notes and afterwards, in the dressing room, would tell them in no uncertain manner what they should or shouldn't have done in certain situations.

On the other hand he conveniently forgot appointments that left some of us embarrassed. On several occasions I remember journalists travelling up from London for a previously arranged appointment only to find that Brian was not intending to come to the ground or he'd 'selectively' forgotten all about it. His secretary was left to try pick up the pieces.

I recall the occasion that he invited my mother and I to join the family for Sunday dinner, at his home in Quarndon, but on arrival we found that they were already halfway through their meal, Brian having apparently forgotten all about the invitation extended to us, and he hadn't told his wife Barbara either. Much to our embarrassment at having intruded, we settled for cheese and biscuits in the lounge while they finished off their meal. Don't know what Barbara thought about it all.

He could always remind me of some comments I made in a past discussion which I had long forgotten, but I learned to live with his eccentricities and continued to appreciate his friendship and admire his achievements.

Without him, the club was destined for the Third Division, fast.

Gary Lineker, former England striker and *Match of the Day* host: 'I got a kiss on the cheek.'

The first time I met Brian Clough was at an airport — he was coming out as I was entering. He walked up to me and said 'Young man, you have a lovely smile. Don't ever lose it.' He proceeded to kiss me on the cheek and then walked away.

John Lawson, journalist, who worked closely with Clough during his 18 years at the City Ground: 'You just never knew what was going to happen next.'

When Brian Clough strode purposefully into the City Ground on a chilly January morning in 1975, he attracted the biggest media pack these parts had ever seen. Eager to make an early impression in his welcoming press conference, I obviously asked one too many questions and he looked me straight in the eye and bawled: 'Are you the local journalist? Thought so. Shut your mouth and I'll see you in my office later.'

In the 48 hours that followed I boarded the team bus for a stay at Bisham Abbey and the small matter of his first game in charge – a third-round FA Cup replay against Tottenham at White Hart Lane. Neil Martin's goal gave him lift-off, but back at Bisham Abbey it was 3am before he granted my notebook an audience…and the plethora of quotes that filled the sports pages of the *Nottingham Evening Post* for several days.

In his early days I think I got in his good books by telling him that my Dad, an ardent Sunderland fan, used to take me along to Roker Park as a kid and actually saw him score goals to an adoring public. It was some time before I got round to telling him I was really a Newcastle fanatic.

I'm also sure I endeared myself to him when I came up with the names of John Robertson and Tony Woodcock when he asked if I could mark his card about any players who could play and were not in the team. He never forgot that, and time after time over the years I purred at hearing him tell all and sundry that 'It was John Lawson who put me right about John Robertson.'

But that was just the start of an amazing 18-year period that was as enjoyable as it was enthralling. Day by day you just never knew what was going to happen next.

Watching him at close hand for almost two decades you couldn't fail to be impressed by the special brand of man management that made him stand out from the rest. I've seen him go to work at getting the best out of Trevor Francis, Peter Shilton and John Robertson – but they are not the episodes that immediately come to mind.

Two stories stand out when I'm asked to illustrate what the man was all about.

One concerned Gary Crosby, the wafer thin winger who has become a trusted aide of Brian's son Nigel. He arrived at the City Ground from Grantham, where Martin O'Neill had much to do with his early development.

He was given the chance to play in a trial match on Forest's training pitch along the embankment with his prospective new manager looking critically on. It was a fairly ordinary sort of game until one of the opposition players, running side by side with Crosby, went down in a heap after being tripped.

BC stopped the game and bellowed at the young trialist: 'Did you do that deliberately?'

Over the years I've never got round to asking Crosby how many different thoughts and answers went whizzing through his brain in that couple of seconds. But at the time he drew a deep breath and replied: 'No boss.'

Confirmation that he dropped on the right answer was immediate. 'Just as well because your feet would not have touched the ground in this club again if you had meant it.' The colour flooded back into Crosby's cheeks, he did enough to earn a full-time contract and went on to play 214 games for Forest and score 25 goals.

The other story concerns a youngster whose name I can't remember but who probably didn't get to figure in one senior game under the great man. But he was taught a pretty sharp lesson in his teenage days and will no doubt still recall the incident with a quirky mixture of shame and pride.

I was chatting to Brian in his office one day when he asked for this young apprentice (as they were called in those days) to come in. I offered to leave because there was clearly a mighty b*******ing coming this poor lad's way. But I was told to stay.

I'm not sure now what wrong he had committed, but clearly he needed to be taught a short, sharp lesson. The verbals were as brutal as anything I've witnessed, and the poor lad was reduced to a quivering wreck in no time. The tears were rolling down his cheeks, he could hardly speak a word and his head was in danger of becoming acquainted with his knee caps.

At the end of it all BC told him to get out of his sight, but just as the youngster was going out of the door he barked: 'Hey, you…go and get me a goal tomorrow!'

From being utterly and totally demoralised, this lad had been picked off the floor with timing that would have done justice to one of Brian's all-time favourites, Eric Morecambe.

I'm not sure whether the lad got his goal the following day, but he was certainly a better person for the experience and I was left to marvel at an example of man management that was simply *par excellence.*

Colin Shields, Nottingham: 'Brian kept his promise.'

The first time I met Brian was during his first year at Derby County. I had gone down to the Baseball Ground to renew my season ticket. But when I arrived, the club secretary told me that all the season tickets had been sold – including mine. I couldn't believe it. I told him I was far from happy about it. I said that I'd been supporting Derby for many, many years, yet they had sold my seat because all of a sudden people were jumping on the bandwagon and wanted tickets. At that moment, Brian walked in and heard the conversation.

'Can I help you, Sir?' asked Brian. I explained what had happened and Brian arranged for me to have a look at where some remaining seats were available in the ground and to try them out. 'Once you've decided which seats you'd like, come back to me,' said Brian. So I had a look at the various seats – I wasn't particularly happy, but I chose a couple and went back into the office.

'Have you chosen where you'd like to sit?' he asked. I said I had, but that I didn't think my mate, who would sit with me, would be very happy about it. 'Well, this is my guarantee to you,' added Brian. 'Next season, when we all start again, you can have first choice of any seat you want.' That sealed it for me. Having felt very despondent that my seats had gone, I left the ticket office that day absolutely elated. And to be fair to Brian, he kept his promise. The following season I got my original seats back.

Chris Williamson, Derby North MP and former leader of Derby City Council: 'A day to remember – and a kiss on the cheek.'

I had the privilege of meeting Brian after writing to ask if he would accept the Freedom of the City of Derby. Unbeknown to me, at the time of writing, Brian was seriously ill and awaiting a liver transplant. It was therefore particularly moving to see him accepting the Freedom of the City accolade.

He had been my schoolboy hero and on the morning of the ceremony I couldn't quite believe I was actually going to meet him. I remember the pride I felt when I was a kid that Brian had taken the club I had been watching play mediocre Second Division football to be one of the best club teams in Europe, if not the world.

But it was with a sense of trepidation that I drove to Brian's house on the morning of the ceremony, prior to the formalities of installing him as Freeman of Derby. But my anxieties were misplaced because Brian surpassed my expectations. He'd lost none of his charm and wit.

We took Brian on a tour of the city before the formal council meeting that was being hosted by Derby County at Pride Park. It was a truly wonderful experience to see him interacting with the thousands of people who lined the route. The tour took in the old Baseball Ground where he regaled me with tales about some of the greatest occasions in the club's history. This included the night we beat Benfica 3–0 in the European Cup – a match I'd watched from the old Pop Side.

But the moment I treasure most about that day was when Brian called me over after the formalities were concluded – when he embraced and kissed me on the cheek. He truly was a terrific hero and a great man who never forgot his roots and stayed true to his socialist principles throughout his life. We will never see his like again.

Norman Giller, journalist and author: 'When Brian hit the right note.' Clough was God's gift to journalists, and nobody knew how to play the power of the press better than he. Cloughie was not so much a spin doctor as a spin surgeon.

I remember noting just how aware he was of the importance of publicity the first time I interviewed him for the *Daily Express*, weeks after he had taken over at Derby in 1967. As we stood chatting, full-back Ron Webster knocked on his office door.

'Got a second, Brian…?' he asked. 'Hey, Young Man, who d'you think you're talking to?' Cloughie shot back. 'To you it's Mister Clough.' He indicated me: 'This Young Man can call me Brian 'cos he's a member of the Fourth Estate, which can do me and this club the power of good. But to you, I'm either Mr Clough or Boss.'

I scripted and co-produced a 1990s documentary for ITV called *Over the Moon, Brian*, which featured Brian Moore looking back over his commentating career.

We took the cameras to Clough's Derbyshire home for the final interview. Unbeknowns to Mooro, I had organised a framed cartoon drawing of him surrounded by the autographs of every major living British footballer, including legends such as Matthews, Finney, Best, Law and Charlton.

The idea was for Cloughie to come in unannounced to make the presentation as Brian was wrapping the programme.

The night before the shoot we spent a pleasant – if a little confusing – evening at the Clough home with Barbara and Brian.

I was accompanied by director and co-producer Brian Klein, which meant there were three Brians in their lounge. Cloughie insisted on playing his latest Sinatra album and singing along with it in a passable imitation of Ol' Blue Eyes.

We shot the main interview in his garden the next day. While Mooro prepared to do his sign-off to camera, Cloughie went off secretly to collect the framed cartoon.

As Brian delivered his closing words in his usual professional style, Cloughie suddenly appeared from behind a hedge carrying the frame. To the surprise of everybody, he made his entrance singing – Sinatra-style – Cole Porter's *You're the Top*.

He sang the whole song, sitting on the knee of a bewildered Brian Moore, and finishing by saying: 'Mr Sinatra and Mr Porter say it much better than I ever can, Brian. You're the top.'

Cue closing titles.

The last time I saw Cloughie was in September 2001, at the funeral and combined celebration-of-life for Brian Moore. I had been sitting at home just over a week earlier watching England destroying Germany 5–1 in Munich when I got a telephone call during the match from Simon Moore, telling me his Dad had died following a heart problem.

I was privileged to be trusted with the eulogy to my good friend, paying respects to Moore the man, while Bob Wilson beautifully and emotionally talked about Moore the broadcaster.

As I looked down on the congregation (400 shoe-horned into the Kent country church with hundreds listening outside) my gaze fell on those trademark George Robey eyebrows of the one and only Cloughie, and I managed to ad-lib how pleased Mooro would have been to see him there. Cloughie was seriously ill, and he had made a monumental effort to get to the service, with Barbara, as ever, at his side.

Brian and I briefly hugged outside the church. 'Well done, Young Man,' he said. 'You did our Brian proud. But if I'd been in that pulpit, I would have sung *You're the Top...*'

You can't top that.

Darren Nunn, York: 'A special proposal.'

I'll always remember the day I met Brian – it was the day I proposed to my wife. I planned to propose to Sam on the scoreboards at Nottingham Forest during a tour of the ground.

When we arrived, Sam was feeling ill with morning sickness, and when we got to the ground a big Mercedes was pulling up outside. As the door opened Brian got out and walked into the reception. I was in a right state from this moment. I was a gibbering wreck; poor Sam had to calm me down.

I had secretly sorted out with a lady at the ground that we would arrive early and we could walk out onto the pitch, where the scoreboards would show my proposal, but seeing Cloughie had thrown me. We ran into the reception where Brian was having photographs taken with his new bust. I stood in awe, with my camera shaking in my hand. I waited a while then asked him if I could have my photo taken with him. He looked across at me and said 'Is this lovely lady with you?' pointing at Sam. When I said 'yes' he said 'I'll have one with both of you if you don't mind, young man.' He had actually called *me* young man.

We stood with him for a while then I remembered why we were there. I walked over to the reception and was told by the lady to go out onto the pitch. After Sam had agreed to marry me we were taken into an office, where a bottle of champagne from Brian was waiting for us. What a lovely man.

I sent a copy of all our favourite photos of the day to him, addressed Brian Clough, Quarndon. Within a week they were all sent back beautifully signed to us, and a few months later, on my birthday, a birthday card was sent to me as well. As with all Forest fans, I feel he is – and always will be – our ultimate hero, and thankfully we have a lasting memory with the amazing statue in Nottingham city centre.

Mike Simpson, Breaston, Derbyshire: 'He told me off for listening-in to his team talk!'

I didn't get off to the best of starts when I met Brian Clough for the first time. I got a right telling off! A friend of mine used to try to listen to the half-time team talk at the City Ground. If you knew where to stand, you could hear what was being said in the Forest dressing room.

So on this particular Saturday, at half-time, we were standing next to the window of the dressing rooms at the back of the Main Stand. We could hear talking and then suddenly Cloughie's head popped out of the window, and he threatened to have us escorted from the ground if we didn't move. I know we shouldn't have been there. It was a bit cheeky really, but I'll always remember that.

Many years later, we met again – this time it was on much better terms. It was at his book signing session at Asda in Spondon. I told him that I remembered seeing him play for Middlesbrough against Forest. He even shook hands with my son Benjamin, a moment we captured on camera for posterity. I'm so glad we had that photo with him. It was a day I'll never forget.

I've always admired Cloughie and all his achievements. I went on to become part of the small committee which raised money for the Brian Clough statue in Nottingham. That came about after I was approached by Marcus, who has compiled this book. It was an extremely proud moment to see the sculpture unveiled by Mrs Clough.

Jimmy Pell, former Nottingham Forest vice-chairman: 'We celebrated promotion with fish and chips.'

I'll never forget being with Brian Clough the day we were promoted to the old First Division back in 1977. Clough had booked 22 places for a break in Cala Millor in Majorca. We were due to fly out there as Bolton were playing Wolves. We'd completed all our matches and were third in the division. Bolton needed to win just three points out of four in their last two games, in order to beat us to the third promotion spot. So Bolton required at least a point against Wolves to keep their hopes alive.

We arrived at East Midlands Airport at half past two, along with the team – minus Larry Lloyd who wouldn't put his blazer on! I was the only director invited by Clough on this occasion. The flight took off at three-o-clock, with an announcement from the captain: 'I'm very pleased to welcome on board the Nottingham Forest team.' Then at 3.20pm, while we were in the air, we heard that Bolton were losing 1–0. We knew that if that continued, Forest would be promoted. But then we went out of radio contact and couldn't follow the score.

We arrived in Palma and I phoned home. My mum said 'Something's happened to Forest,' but she didn't know the full details. Eventually, Cloughie managed to phone home, and it was confirmed that we were promoted. We stayed in Cala Millor, and at about two-o-clock in the morning John McGovern and I went out to get 22 packets of fish and chips to celebrate.

The next day, I was relaxing in the sunshine when Clough and Taylor came up to me and said: 'You've got promoted, now it better be Shilton, Gemmill and Burns before we kick-off the new season.' I felt like I was sitting in quick sand! Just the thought of it! But of course we signed Peter Shilton, Archie Gemmill and Kenny Burns before Christmas and we went on to win the Championship.

John McGovern, Brian Clough's European Cup-winning captain (twice) at Nottingham Forest, who also played for him at Hartlepool, Derby County and Leeds United: 'The day he gave me some advice about my hairstyle.'

I first signed for Brian at Hartlepool, when I was a youngster. It was back in the 1960s, and I wanted my hair long because, if I wasn't going to make it as a footballer, I wanted to be a rock star – I was a big Mick Jagger fan and would loved to have followed him. The gaffer asked me about my hair one day, and I said something like 'George Best has it this way.' His answer was: 'When you can play like George Best you can grow your hair like him! Get it cut.' There was no compromise.

Brian was one of the best teachers of the game that there's ever been. He might have sounded a complicated person to a lot of people, but his philosophy was very simple and straight forward about most things in life.

When it came to football it was all about getting the basics right, like passing the ball to a teammate. Before you could do that you had to win it, and he told all his players to treat it as a friend and not to lose it.

If ever I need memories of Brian, I just have to look at the medals in my cabinet at home – it's full of them.

Paul Garton: 'Brian invited us into his office.'

I used to attend Mundella Grammar School in the Meadows area of Nottingham, and most lunchtimes a friend and I would go to the City Ground to collect players' autographs after training. One particular day, Brian Clough returned from squash, and we asked him for his autograph (I used to have photos in a book, and the players and staff used to sign them). He responded with 'Follow me, lads' and proceeded to take us into his office.

The office was full of journalists, and we assumed it was some sort of press conference. Mr Clough told me and my friend to sit in the two chairs in front of his desk, while he signed all the pictures we wanted. All this time that we were sitting in his office, all the journalists stood around waiting for him to finish with us. It made us feel very important, and he asked us a lot of questions – especially why we weren't at school. He also passed on some words of wisdom about my spots! (I used to have a lot of them). He told me to go home and get 'yer Mam' to boil some cabbage water for me to drink. He was certain it would clear my spots up. I did try it, but unfortunately it didn't work.

We were completely in awe while in his presence, and to this day remember the meeting like it was yesterday (it would be about 35 years ago now). I feel sure no modern-day manager would give us as much time as he did that day and, true to form, no one could emulate him as a person or a motivator. What a great man!

Keith Daniell, former TV and radio journalist: 'The day Brian returned to management – with a team of schoolchildren.'
After Brian retired I came up with the idea of reuniting him with former rivals and players in a series for ITV.

Needless to say, Brian was a natural performer and his reunion with Martin O'Neill and John Robertson was fascinating. With other programmes, Brian led the conversations. With Martin and Robbo, there was a deference and respect resembling that of schoolboys summoned to see the headmaster.

But my best memory of that series – and all my moments with Brian over 20 years as a journalist in radio and television – was his return to management!

For a Christmas special Brian was the boss again – of East Bridgford Primary School in Nottinghamshire. These youngsters had barely heard of Brian Clough – and yet he was the communicator supreme. First we put him in front of a class of 10-year-olds for a question and answer session.

One asked Brian how to become a better player. Brian got a tennis ball out of his pocket.

'If I throw this to you what are you going to do?' asked Brian.

'Catch it,' said young Aaron.

'Then what?' said Brian.

'Er. I'll throw it to Tom so he can catch it.'

'And what will Tom do?' asked Brian.

'He'll throw it to James to catch it.'

'So,' Brian said. 'When you play football keep the ball. Treat it as something you love and value. When you get the ball don't kick it away. Pass it to one of your mates so he can look after it. And then he'll pass it to one of his mates. Just look after the ball.'

The team went out and played a special match for Brian. With 200 children cheering on, Brian told the centre-forward to stay upfront. Twice the player drifted back.

'Centre-forward,' shouted Brian. 'If you do that again you're off.' We were only five minutes into the match!

The centre-forward drifted back again. Brian substituted him!

My wife, Alison, who has no interest in football, was sitting with Brian afterwards in the staffroom having a cup of tea. Brian asked her if we had children.

'Two daughters', Alison told him.

'I bet one's a villain,' said Cloughie, who then spent the next 20 minutes asking about our family.

In that one moment Alison was as captured by Brian's personality as those of us who worshipped him for his football genius.

John Dickie: 'Brian Clough confiscated my scarf.'

I'm a Stoke fan, and as a 'young man' (aged 16) I went with my best mate from school to see Stoke's first away match of the 1979–80 season. We'd just been promoted to the First Division and our hosts were the newly crowned European champions. By some freakish piece of luck, the tickets we got were over the tunnel at the City Ground.

When the teams came out for the game, I dangled my scarf over the edge of the tunnel, and most of the players patted it when they came out. It was a particularly big thrill because Forest were parading the European Cup at the time. And the thrill was complete – or so I thought – when Brian Clough came out after the teams and tugged on the scarf.

I did the same thing just after the half-time whistle, with the same result. But then, while I was distracted for a second by something my friend said, my scarf disappeared out of my hand. I looked down and there was Brian Clough with my scarf. He put two fingers up towards me, said, 'That's twice,' and then disappeared into the tunnel. Forest went on to win the game 1–0 (I think).

A few days later I wrote to Mr Clough, saying how much I admired Forest's passing game (creepy, I know, but true), and asking for my scarf back. It was duly returned to me together with an autographed photo: 'To John, "Be Good," Brian Clough.' I still treasure the picture.

Gary Newbon, TV presenter: 'Of all my interviewees – he was at the top.'

It would take me forever to pay tribute to Brian Clough. He had a massive influence on my career. Over 42 years in television I've interviewed so many people, but I put Brian Clough up there as the Number One. I never knew what was going to happen on the interviews, but I knew he was going to have a fantastic impact with the various audiences which were listening to these interviews, because he was so outrageous at times.

I was seriously ill about eight years ago. I don't think Brian wrote many letters, but when I came out of hospital after 15 long days, the first letter I opened was a hand-written letter from Brian Clough which said 'Be Good, we love you – Brian and Barbara Clough.' And I've got that framed – it was something special. He was a very special man, and it was a great honour when Barbara asked me if I'd compere the unveiling of the statue in Nottingham.

Nora Armstrong, Nottinghamshire: 'My service station encounter with Cloughie.'

I met Brian Clough at a motorway service station late one night. I'm a life-long Forest fan and I'd been travelling back from a mid-week away match at Bristol Rovers. I was with my friend Margaret and I remember it was a bitterly cold night – I had to keep wiping snow off the windscreen with my hand because the wipers had frozen-up! It was a long and frustrating journey, but when I saw the Forest team coach had parked-up at the same service station as us I was absolutely delighted.

It seemed too good an opportunity to miss, so we went to get some autographs. But Brian told the players to get on the coach sharpish, he didn't want them hanging around any longer than they needed to. So I told him that we'd travelled all the way from Nottingham to Bristol and back, to support the team, and it was only right that we should collect a few signatures. At that point, Brian signalled to the players and he lined them up to ensure we got all the autographs we needed, before wishing us a safe journey home. The following morning, Margaret's young son was over the moon with the autographs and became a big fan of Cloughie.

Geraldine Ellis, Nottingham: 'We shared some of his last moments at the City Ground.'

I met Brian Clough during his final hours at the City Ground, back in 1993. His outstanding reign as Nottingham Forest manager had come to an end – and his fans were still eager to show how much he meant to them. It was the night of his last home match, which was actually a reserve game. My son Chris had waited outside the reception area in the hope of seeing him. He was part of a small group which had gathered and they were eventually invited into his office. Chris had phoned me to explain what was happening and I was invited in too. We all shared some precious moments with Brian before he left the City Ground for the last time. He was playing some of his favourite songs by Frank Sinatra. It was a very emotional evening and one we'll never forget.

Garry Birtles, European Cup-winner (twice) at Nottingham Forest: 'No two days were the same.'

One of my first introductions to Brian Clough will always stick in my memory. He gave me a right telling off! I was getting ready for a training session during a month's trial at Forest, and he caught me sitting on the table in the away dressing room. In no uncertain terms, he told me to get off the table. With a growl and a scowl, he'd left me in no doubt who was the boss around there.

When I was in the reserves, I'd often play squash with him, just over the road from the City Ground. I'd have just finished training and would be caked in mud, so I'd do my best to clean myself up and we'd go to the courts at Trent Bridge. We had some really great games. But sometimes I'd bump into him as I was trying to get to a shot. He would ask, 'Do you want to play that point again, son?' What could I say? So I'd reply 'No, it's OK gaffer' and he won the point. He didn't like to lose, whether it was a game of football or a game of squash.

In later years I remember we were due to fly on a Sunday for a match in Kuwait, but I was injured. We were all on the coach to take us to the airport, but I didn't know why I was having to go halfway across the world for a match I couldn't play in.

The gaffer heard me grumbling and asked what the problem was. So I told him I thought it would be better if I stayed and got fit rather than flying to Kuwait. He replied, 'Son, you've got a point there' and he told the driver to stop the coach. We hadn't gone far – we were on Wilford Lane in Nottingham – and he got off the coach and stood in the middle of the road to stop the next car that came along. He asked the driver to take me back to the ground – and so this poor guy did as he was asked. I decided to go to the pub, and it wasn't until later that day that I found out the trip didn't go ahead after all. Ian Wallace told me they'd all got on the plane and it had tried to take off, but the procedure was aborted. The gaffer didn't like flying, and he took the whole team off the plane, marched them across the tarmac and everyone came back. So there was no trip to Kuwait!

Life with the gaffer was so unpredictable – no two days were the same. He even got us running through a clump of nettles in the corner of the training ground. It was like compost corner, where the groundsman dumped all the grass cuttings. You'd then hear him shout, 'last one in the five-a-side net' and everyone would run to the goal and try and squeeze into the net! It was bizarre. It was just another way that the Gaffer showed us who was the boss.

Mark Crossley, former Nottingham Forest goalkeeper: 'He told me to report to his house.'

The gaffer could soon bring us back down to earth when we were doing well. I remember we'd just beaten Southampton at home – it was our third win in a row – and I was in the dressing room getting ready to go. I picked up my bag and said 'See you Monday, lads.' He stood up and shouted over towards me. He ordered me to report to his house first thing the next morning, a Sunday. I walked out the dressing room and then realised I didn't even know where he lived! So I spoke to the groundsman who told me how to get there.

I had to get to his house for 9am. So I set-off at quarter to six – just to make sure I was there in plenty of time! I parked-up outside his house for about an hour and I kept thinking 'What am I going to say when I knock on his door?' Anyway, Barbara came to the door, let me in and made me a cup of tea. He appeared about 10 minutes later.

'Thank you,' he said. I was mystified. 'What for?' I asked. 'For agreeing to play for our Simon's team today.' What could I say to that? 'Ah, no problem at all,' was my reply. So, one day I'm playing in the top level of professional football against Southampton. The next, I'm appearing in Division Five of the Derbyshire Sunday League. We won 4–0. But later I found out they got the points taken off them and were nearly kicked out of the League for playing a ringer! But looking back over the years, I'll always be very grateful for what the gaffer did for me – without him my career wouldn't have happened.

Brian Laws, former Nottingham Forest player: 'Brian's surprise question.'

My fondest memory of Brian Clough is on our first meeting prior to me signing for Nottingham Forest from Middlesbrough. Cloughie asked me on arriving, 'Can you tell me if you are a good player or a bad player?' I was shocked by his question and replied 'You must know that I'm a good player because you wouldn't want to sign me otherwise.' Brian replied, 'Stop being a smart arse and answer the question.' So I replied, 'Yes, I am a good player.' Clough commented: 'We will soon find out 'cause I have never seen you play, so if you are a good player you tell everybody Cloughie signed you, but if you are rubbish then somebody else signed you!'

Pete Masters: 'I rescued Brian Clough's canary.'

During my holidays from university in the scorching summer of 1975, I got a splendid job 'putty bashing' at Arbo Sealants, in Belper, Derbyshire. One teatime, I was making my way home, as white and dusty as a flour grader, up Ferrers Way in Derby, when I spotted something bright yellow on the pavement. Close inspection revealed it to be an exhausted canary.

I gently carried the little chap home and after a few days of seed and water he had executed a remarkable recovery. Unfortunately, by now, my Mum was giving me terrible earache over the mess he was making and finally, in spite of all my protestations, she issued me with an ultimatum for his removal.

After considerable trouble and rejections from a couple of local fanciers, I finally fixed the lad up with a brave new life at the home of my mate's Mum. But on the same day I read in the *Derby Evening Telegraph*: 'Lost – one canary, Ferrers Way area.'

I rang the number and the man said he would be round shortly. Five minutes later, a Mercedes pulled up and out got Brian Clough with Simon, Elizabeth and Nigel in tow.

The canary was duly identified as Tarzan, and restored to the Clough family.

My friend's Mum gracefully declined my offer to buy her a replacement, and I thought that was the end of the story. However, two nights later Brian appeared with a large box of Milk Tray for my Mum, who dined out for years on the tale of how we found Brian Clough's canary.

Mike Hunter, Ocala, Florida, United States: 'He even outshone Elton John.'

I was serving with Hertfordshire Police, and I wrote to Brian saying I would like to meet him at Nottingham Forest, and he phoned my house (I thought it was a wind up at first), and he invited myself and my wife up to a game against Everton and some subsequent matches. He was the true professional and gentleman that everyone now knows him to be. We spent time in his office with him and Peter Taylor and he introduced us to Trevor Francis (just signed). Each visit after that he was all we had imagined him to be – larger than life with an immediate command of respect that came from his professionalism, not from fear as some would say.

We met again when he came to Watford FC, as he was commentating on the game, and I was on motor cycle duty escorting Elton John to the ground as he was chairman – but Brian even managed to outshine Elton! Great days. Brian had that aura about him that endeared you to him immediately, and our whole family miss him and his repartee...there will never be another.

I visited Brian quite a few times and on one occasion my wife had flu...so Brian said 'what does she like to drink?' I said she did not drink so he took a great big pot plant in a copper container out of his office and said 'Give her this with a kiss from me.' I said I was not walking through Nottingham with something that size, so he had a guy drive me back to my car in his Mercedes, together with the plant. Further more, he made sure that I had a car park pass in future! He was a true gentleman and extremely generous.

Peter Thygesen, Denmark: 'Brian gave me a tip – of almost an entire day's pay!'

Back in 1974, I was working as an assistant manager at the Magnum Hotel, situated not far from the A1 between Newcastle and Whitley Bay. At that time Derby County were due to play Sunderland in (I guess) a Cup tournament. So they stayed at the hotel.

The match ended with a draw, so a replay had to take place three days later. After the first match, the team arrived back rather late at the hotel. Everything was in fact closed. But the guys were hungry, so even though I was a liquor manager, I went to the main kitchen and made a Danish speciality, named 'English Steak,' which no one had ever heard about in the British Isles. It's simply a pan-fried steak, served with soft, brown, fried onions and gravy from the pan. And they liked it a lot.

Brian Clough – it must have been him – gave me a tip of £5, equal to almost a day's salary for me. The hotel had a football team for female staff only. In order to kill some time, a match between Derby County and the female staff-team was arranged. Unfortunately, I didn't see it, as that afternoon I had to go into Newcastle. But when I returned to the hotel later that day, I learned that our women had won!

Martin Sowerby, a rugby fan from Wakefield, West Yorkshire: 'I won't forget our meeting in the Leeds United car park.'

I was very lucky to meet Brian in 1974 during his short stay at Leeds United. I was a 10-year-old Barnsley supporter and was taken to a Leeds game by service bus, as we always did in those days, by my father. I arrived very early that day and was not too bothered about the game, but my Dad loved his football and would watch anyone if Barnsley were playing away and he could not get there.

I was walking across the old car park, at which point my Dad said to me 'Look, there's Cloughie.' I asked, 'Who's that?' I was told it was Brian Clough, the Leeds manager. Dad said I should go and get his autograph. He pulled out his pen for filling in the programme, gave me a betting slip – of all things – and off I trotted.

I shouted: 'Mr Clough, can I have your autograph please? It's for my Dad.' Brian looked over at my Dad, then looked at me, winked and smiled. Brian gave me the autograph and asked me if I played football.

I was speechless that the manager of Leeds wanted to know if I played football. There was only the three of us in the car park and I was very nervous.

'No,' I said, 'I come from Wakefield.'

'Don't they play football in Wakefield?' asked Brian.

'Yes, but I play rugby.' To which Brian said the words that only later did I understand – and will never forget: 'You'll fit in well around here.'

I never forgot that meeting and years later, when I was 16, I had the pleasure of watching him prove to the world what a gifted, talented and special man he was. God bless you, Brian.

Andy Heathfield: 'In strode Brian, taking us all by surprise.'

I'll never forget the day Brian Clough made a surprise visit. It was in Melbourne, a small village eight miles south of Derby, which had a men's club aligned with the local Baptist Church. They used to invite people to speak for a very small fee.

In the early Clough days at Derby County, the men's club invited midfielder Alan Durban to attend and give a talk – 'life as a professional footballer.' I was lucky enough to be taken by my father.

The start time of 7pm went by, and by 7.30pm the club officials were getting worried. Just then, into the room strode Brian Clough who opened with the remark: 'Durban's been injured in training today, and I've told him that he can't be here, so you're stuck with me instead.'

There then followed 90 minutes of tales, stories and anecdotes from the great man himself, who also 'borrowed' a few cigarettes along the way as he enthralled the audience. He happily answered our questions including, 'Why can't winger Alan Hinton [nicknamed Gladys] tackle?' Back came the answer: 'Because I pay him to score goals and deliver crosses.'

Then with a 'That's your lot, I'm off,' he went. The committee tried to pay him a fee, but he would have none of it. He got into his car and drove off. A truly memorable night.

Jimmy Pell, former Nottingham Forest vice-chairman: 'Clough sat next to me in the Directors' Box.'
Brian Clough was a very generous man. Whenever I had a charity to support and needed a financial donation, he would always

arrange to do a newspaper article for me and make sure that the cheque from the newspaper went straight to the charity concerned.

He also bought some red roses for my Mum so she could put them in a glass vase which had been specially commissioned for one of our Cup successes. I've also got a lovely replica of the European Cup made from Waterford glass – again, that was specially commissioned.

Six months after he was appointed manager, I was elected onto the Forest board by the members. I met him for the first time at the annual meeting. Initially, I got to know him at the board meetings – when he occasionally honoured us with his presence!

Clough would sometimes come into the Forest board room – but only occasionally. We'd be dressed properly in suits and ties, entertaining the visiting directors after a match, and he'd be wearing his green sweater.

I remember that when he got a touchline ban, he sat next to me in the Directors' Box. He was shouting and bellowing at the players – I thought it was best to sit there and say nothing!

But when he used to phone me at the office, he would say 'It's Brian here,' and I would reply 'Brian who?' just to pull his leg!

On one occasion he phoned me before we were due to play in the UEFA Cup against Celtic at the City Ground. It was a night match, and during the day it had been bitterly cold. Brian rang me and said: 'Get down here.'

'What's the matter, Brian?' I asked him.

He said: 'We've got problems with the Spanish referee.'

'Well, what can I do about it?' I asked.

'Get down here,' he insisted.

So I went down to the ground, and the Spanish referee was inspecting the pitch. It was freezing, even in the middle of the afternoon, and I was wearing a sheepskin coat. All the Celtic fans were parked-up in buses near the ground, and there was no way we could cope with about 12,000 Celtic supporters going rampant in Nottingham.

Clough came out to the side of the pitch and said: 'It's alright, we can play in this.'

But the referee was looking very doubtful. Eventually, the UEFA representative turned-up, and he was from Finland – it was almost like a summer's day to him. So the game went ahead.

After the second leg, we flew back from Glasgow to East Midlands Airport in a small plane called a Fokker Friendship. But Brian didn't like the look of it and refused to get on. Anyway, we managed to persuade him – and I told him: 'It's OK Brian, once we're flying, it's all down hill, so it won't be too bad!'

Tony Smith, Hayle, Cornwall: 'It was like meeting God.'

I was a security officer at ATV, and the boiler man at the studios (Percy) said he was a great friend of Peter Taylor and Brian, and if ever I wanted to see a game he would arrange everything. I didn't need asking twice and the following week I drove him up to Nottingham for a game against Southampton. We drove into the car park, and Percy took me into the reception area and told me to take a seat. After a short period he returned and asked me to follow him down a corridor and into an office on the left-hand side, and there, sitting at his desk, was Mr Clough.

It was like meeting God. He introduced himself (as if he had to!) and asked if we wanted a beer. We then chatted for at least 10 minutes, and in that time his secretary came in and said the Head of Sport at ATV would like to see him. He told her to usher him into one of the other offices and he would see him when he had finished talking to his quests. It was great for us – the boiler man and security officer – keeping the Head of Sport at our company waiting! On leaving, Percy was able to take me to the dressing rooms and out on the pitch, all on Brian's say so. For lunch, we went to an Italian restuarant very close to Trent Bridge where we had lunch with a former Derby County director. After the game, many of the players, including Peter Shilton, spoke to Percy and myself. It was a wonderful day and, thanks to Brian, one I will never forget.

Kenny Burns, European Cup-winner (twice) at Nottingham Forest: 'He was like an adopted father to me.'

One of the first times I met him was when he took me to a garden centre for a sweet pea show – but up until then the only pea I knew about was the mushy variety! He had a sweet pea named after him. But, coming from Scotland, I didn't really know anything about flowers. On another occasion, I went to ask him for a week off so I could get married. He said 'OK' – and added that he would come to the wedding too. I'm pleased to say he made a special effort for the wedding – he got new laces for his trainers!

He was like an adopted father to me. I was only 22 or 23 years old when I joined him at Nottingham Forest. He told you what to do and what not to do. He was like a Dad – when he said something, you listened and you did it.

He once fined me for making a bad pass across the defence, which was nearly cut-out by the opposition. He fined me £50, and I took my punishment. He also fined me £50 for head-butting another player on the back of the head, and I was caught on camera. Again, I learned my lesson and took the punishment.

When he retired, I went to see him at his house. He'd be lying on the settee with a blanket around him, and Barbara would make us a cup of tea. We'd talk about the good old days.

It was a huge shock when he passed away. I feel sorry for anyone who never had the chance to meet him. Whether you liked the way he said things or not, you were always a better person for having met him.

Colin Tarrant, the actor who played Brian Clough in the tribute play *Old Big 'Ead in the Spirit of the Man*: 'It was a dream come true.'
To have the opportunity to play my hero, Brian Clough, on stage was absolutely wonderful. It was a dream come true. It's one of those jobs that you think will never happen. And then all of a sudden – one day – I'm reading the local newspaper and there's an article about plans for a Brian Clough play at the local theatre. I couldn't believe my eyes. I got in touch with my agent and said I've got to be put forward for that.

When I was younger I used to do impressions of Mr Clough, along with Peter Cook too. I'm a Nottingham Forest supporter –

my eldest brother is also a lifelong fan – and I used to stand in the Trent End. So to perform in front of all those great players at the Gala Performance at the Nottingham Playhouse was terrific. It was a full house and a night I will never forget.

The play was a massive task – in fact, it was a play within a play. It was quite nerve-wracking at first, but after the first week I became more comfortable and it was a wonderful play to be part of. I was also delighted to meet Brian Clough's family. That was a real privilege.

Rob Banner, Derby: 'He made sure I ate all my tomatoes.'
I grew up with Brian's sons Nigel and Simon as best friends. Brian was often like a Dad to me. I spent more time at their house than my own – and the City Ground as well. My fondest memory is when he made me eat tomatoes. I hated them but was not allowed to leave the table until my plate was empty. I saw him sit down with a huge cigar that Peter Taylor gave him and just stare at the switched off TV, which just happened to have the European Cup on it.

I remember his generosity to almost everyone – the school fêtes and church fayres he attended, taking his trophies to show to the local cub scouts and even the schools which Nigel and Simon didn't go to.

Brian refereed several local boys matches, and it had a tremendous effect on so many youngsters. He refereed Ferrers Way (our team) verses Portreath Drive – it was all the local lads that met up at the field nearest to our homes. We were lucky enough to wear the Forest youth team's away kit and bring in a couple of ringers, who would be cousins Tony and Neil.

The matches were played on the old rugby ground on Keddleston Road. It was a really big thing for us, lads aged between about 10 and 15, and the best manager in the world. It was quite scary, but he encouraged us all and we all went home with smiles even if we lost.

Stephen Rawlinson, Hertfordshire: 'I got a phone call at 2am – it was none other than Brian Clough.'
Back in 1991, Brian Clough was in London for a few days filming a TV commercial for a breakfast cereal (Shredded Wheat, I think). My brother-in-law was the restaurant and bar manager at the hotel where he was staying and got talking about the great Forest team of the late Seventies. Once he mentioned that I was a big Forest fan, Brian said that he would be delighted to meet me after he had returned from the match against Newcastle the following evening (an FA Cup fourth-round replay).

The following evening, both myself and my wife waited patiently at the hotel until just after midnight. With no sign of him arriving, we made our way home a little disappointed. Shortly after 2am the telephone rang. It was my brother-in-law, who said he had someone who wanted to speak to me...it was none other than Brian Clough! I might have been half asleep when the phone rang, but I was wide awake now – this wasn't a dream. He made his apologies about not getting back earlier and missing the opportunity to meet me, but was clearly pleased that Forest had made it through to the next round of the FA Cup. We talked football for a few minutes until it was time to say goodbye. I was eternally grateful that he went out of his way to speak to me, and it shows that he was a genuine man of the people.

It was some years later at a book signing for *Cloughie – Walking on Water* in Cheapside, London, that I came face to face with Brian Clough. I stood in line nervously waiting my turn, using the time to think about what I would say when I eventually got to meet him. We shook hands and he asked me my name. I then proceeded to recall the time when he telephoned me at home. He gave me a wry smile and then completely caught me off-guard with his question: 'Did it make you want to buy the cereal?' Clearly referring to the TV commercial. To which I replied 'No.' He made a comment that it was just as well he had stuck to football then. I'm sure that most football fans would agree.

Kay Hudson, Nottingham: 'My day with Brian was unforgettable.'
I was fortunate enough to spend the day with the 'Big Man' in 2002 to organise the launch of his second autobiography, *Walking on Water*. I was both anxious and excited to meet Brian and thought the day was either going to be a nightmare, a day of challenges or unbelievable fun. Luckily for me it was the latter, and I was his 'young lady' for the day.

Over 8,000 people queued in the City Ground car park in an orderly manner to buy their book from the club shop and to meet the man whose persona commanded respect and made most people stand to attention. There was a real buzz around the ground and everyone was pleased to see him and to reminisce about the good old times.

One of my favourite memories of the day was my initial meeting with Brian to discuss the day's itinerary. Once we had agreed on the plan of action for the day – and established we got on just fine – I decided to have a little fun. I introduced a colleague of mine who was the camera man on the day, Andy Fairey. Brian's reaction was 'Fairey? Is he a poof?'

He was warm, charming, quick witted, often his tongue was quite loose but that was just his way of dealing with people and things. I don't think he meant any malice or offence to anyone he met – he just had the tendency to say what he thought, which as you can imagine was completely not politically correct, but sometimes very amusing. At the end of a long day, he gave me a hug and a kiss and thanked me for all my help. He went home with an aching hand (from signing all the books) while I went home with aching feet from running around all day making sure everything went smoothly. It was a day I'll never forget.

Mick Sharp, Chaddesden, Derby: 'Reading Cloughie's electric meter.'

I met Brian just once – at his home in Quarndon, when I went to read the electric meter. I asked him if he minded me talking about football, and he said 'What's your name, young man?' I replied, 'Mick'. He pondered and called me Michael. It amused me that he wouldn't call me Mick. I just thanked him for the pleasure he had given people with Derby and Forest and said he should have been England manager – to which he thanked me and agreed, of course, about the England job.

I didn't stay long as I was aware of encroaching on his private time. He was on the TV doing the adverts for the electricity board about Economy 7 at the time. The other meter readers said that he often gave them a box of chocolates when they called. I didn't get a box of chocs – but my treat was simply to meet him, a memory I still treasure today.

Peter J. Smith: 'Two sugars please, Mr Clough.'

I had the pleasure of tending his lawns for many years after he had a lawn machine bought for him one Christmas. He asked a friend of mine who maintained his trees, if he could operate the new machine he'd just had. My friend said, no, he couldn't – but he knew a man who could. That's when I had an invitation to meet the great man.

On the morning of meeting him, I got up early, cleaned my old battered truck and set off in plenty of time, so I wasn't late, as I knew he liked people to be on time. When I arrived at his house in Quarndon, I left my truck on the roadside, outside his house, because I was afraid of my truck spilling oil on his driveway. As you can gather, I was in awe of the great man before I ever met him, due to his media reputation.

As I got near the house I could see some people inside, but ventured around to the back door and knocked and waited nervously. There was a great commotion behind the door with Del Boy the dog and his famous master telling him to be quiet (or words to that effect). The door flung open and there he was, dressed in his familiar Umbro jacket, blue tracksuit bottoms and tatty trainers. He stared at me and said 'You must be Peter, how many sugars in your coffee?' I stuttered my reply, 'Two please Mr Clough.' He pointed his famous finger at me and said 'Brian, call me Brian.' I replied, 'Two, Mr Brian.'

From that day, I struck up a good impression and I got the job of maintaining his lawns for many years.

Mark Shardlow, BBC journalist: 'I hosted his first-ever radio phone-in.'

I was 18 when I first met Brian Clough. I commentated on Nottingham Forest for Hospital Radio. And I was down at the City Ground to record a feature interview with the great man. I waited in reception with the more experienced reporters from the national press and BBC radio. His secretary, Carole, came out and called me in first. I couldn't believe it. But I later found out to expect the unexpected with Cloughie.

It was a bitterly cold Friday in December. 'You look freezing!' he said as I went into his office. 'Let me get you a drink.' And on he went to pour a whiskey. He gave me a great 15-minute interview and wished me every success in my career. I left floating on air, to be greeted with the worn faces of the press still waiting in reception. Some years later, I'd understand how they felt.

I became sports producer at BBC Radio Nottingham in 1988. Friday was interview day at Forest. But there was no set time. I'd be down at the ground by 9am. Mr Clough would rarely give interviews at this time. And his players followed suit. We had to hang around outside, hoping to catch a player before training. With luck, Brian Laws or Neil Webb would oblige. But often we were told to return after training – which could finish as early as 11:30. We then might have to wait for them to have their lunch. And sometimes we would leave at 1pm with nothing. I could think back to my hospital radio interview and now understand the weary look of the press pack.

But when Brian spoke it was gold dust. Brilliant, witty and incisive. Like few others in football. And those hours of waiting were sometimes handsomely rewarded. After an FA Cup win at

Watford my colleague went down more in hope than expectation of getting an interview. He came back with quotes from the manager, 11 players, sub and travelling reserves. Brian had taken him into the dressing room and escorted him from player to player.

My last interview with Brian Clough was something of an historic moment. I was working for BBC *East Midlands Today* but presented Brian's first-ever radio phone-in. He was not a particularly well man – a much frailer figure than the man I first met. The mind, though, was as sharp as ever. And I certainly had to keep my wits about me as he skirted the line of libel and reason with his typically forthright comments.

'The ugliest player I ever signed was Kenny Burns,' he told one fan who asked him to name his best signing.

'Hiya beauty,' was Cloughie's greeting to a young woman who called the hour-long phone-in. She asked for his opinion on the controversial UEFA Cup semi-final against Anderlecht in 1984.

'The referee cheated us from start to finish,' he replied.

He also spoke about David Platt's foreign signings for Forest.

'I can't even spell spaghetti never mind talk Italian. How could I tell an Italian to get the ball – he might grab mine.'

And on it went. I can claim another first for that day, too. I asked Brian if I could record a TV interview. He happily obliged. But as the camera was about to roll he called a halt. 'Hey!' he said 'I can't go on TV without a tie.' He took a fancy to mine. So off it came, and Brian carefully tied it around his neck. And so Brian Clough appeared on TV wearing my tie.

Dan Norton, Scarborough: 'He told us to eat our vegetables.'

I met Mr Clough (as I was asked to address him) as a young boy of eight. My brother and I were in the City Ground car park obtaining autographs from players in our school holidays. He took us into his office through a side door and asked us a few questions and gave us both a signed picture. He also told us to eat what our Mam gave us, including the veg! He was a remarkable man and I always felt that whenever I entered the City Ground it was his Kingdom. I miss his character and his up-front manner.

Douglas Martin, York City fan: 'Cloughie left me speechless.'

In December 1986 I travelled from York to watch Newcastle play Nottingham Forest in a First Division game. I had never been to Newcastle's ground before, nor had I seen either team play before.

But the main reason I was going to the match was to see 'Brian Clough's' Nottingham Forest. I was simply inspired by the aura of the man and what he had achieved with Forest. Yes, they were in transition when I saw them, but they were still holding their own in the League and always tried to play proper passing football. His achievements, at both Forest and Derby, were like a *Roy of the Rovers* story.

On this winter's day, I went into the ground early and stood on the terrace under the old main stand and noticed that the man himself was being interviewed on the pitch by a TV crew. I don't remember who was interviewing Clough but when he had finished he came running up the terrace right past me – and I stood there like a little girl wanting to say something but was unable to. No words came out of my mouth because I was awe struck. But thankfully Cloughie spoke. 'Enjoy the game, son.' I smiled and nodded but was unable to speak due to stage fright. I suspect that this memory will remain with me until my OAP days.

John Robertson, European Cup-winner (twice) with Cloughie at Nottingham Forest: 'He kept us relaxed – that was the key.'
There's no doubt that without the gaffer I wouldn't have achieved

all the things I have done in football. He kept things simple, and relaxation was important, especially before big matches. I remember that before the second European Cup Final, he took us all to Spain for a few days so we could take it easy in the sunshine. It was like a holiday for us. The trip kept us relaxed, so we weren't sitting worrying about the Final. And of course it worked a treat — we went to the game in the right frame of mind and won the Cup for a second time.

(John was speaking to the author on stage at the civic reception for the Brian Clough statue in Nottingham.)

Steve Berry, Coventry: 'My first Forest match — and I met the great man.'

It was the 1991–92 season — the venue: Coventry City's Highfield Road, as I lived in Coventry. At the age of 12, it was the very first time I had been able to go and see Forest, so I was really excited. My best friend, Leigh, was a Coventry fan so there was friendly banter. We got to the ground at around 2 o'clock, so the guys were out on the pitch warming up at that point. We then spotted that green jumper — it was Brian of course.

We ran down the side of the stands and onto the touchline shouting 'Brian, Brian.' He turned round and said 'Hello.' There was another little boy with his Dad as well. Brian posed for photos and signed autographs, it was brilliant! It was my first Forest match live and I met the great man. As we were finishing, the lads were coming back into the dressing room and we stood by the tunnel waiting for them, holding up our autograph books like the excited little children that we were. They just passed us by, walking towards the dressing room. Someone said they were getting psyched-up for the game. OK, we thought. Then all I heard was...

'ERR YOOUNG MAN!'

Stuart Pearce turned round.

'COME BACK AND SIGN THESE LADS' AUTOGRAPHS!'

At that moment Stuart Pearce, Nigel Clough, Ian Woan and Roy Keane turned round, came over and signed our programmes – then were told to get on their way.

I always wonder to this day whether Roy Keane would have done that for Alex Ferguson. That was the respect the man demanded and, in turn, got. I've never seen anything like it since in my 23 years as a Forest fan (I went on to be a Junior Red for three years and always follow their fortunes now).

KNIGHTHOOD FOR CLOUGHIE

Shortly after my tribute website was set-up, a campaign began to get a Knighthood for Cloughie. I received e-mails from fans all over the world and eventually a petition containing 7,500 names and messages was handed-in at 10 Downing Street in October 2004. Although the campaign had started while Brian was alive, and the date for the Downing Street visit was arranged well in advance, his sad death in September 2004 meant campaigners hoped there would be a posthumous award.

I was accompanied to Downing Street by my wife Sarah and Cloughie's MP, Bob Laxton. We handed-over three volumes of documents showing the support which the campaign had received from fans and famous names including Gary Lineker, John Motson, Sam Allardyce, Trevor Francis and the MP Ken Clarke.

The government's response was that posthumous honours are given only for gallantry. A letter from the Honours Unit said the then Prime Minister, Tony Blair, had sympathised with the aims of the petition. But the letter said the current statutes did not allow Mr Blair to make nominations for posthumous Knighthoods.

Yet the words of one top manager still resound with many fans when he commented about Brian: 'He'll always be a Sir in my eyes.'

For the record, the following few tributes are among the many that were included in the petition handed-in to 10 Downing Street.

'As a young boy living on the next street to the Clough family, I remember Brian very well. We played against each other in competing street teams on Clairville Common. It was Valley Road v Eden Road. I also remember that in our family you couldn't say a bad word against Brian Clough. My late mother was a cleaner at the school Brian attended, and she had nothing but praise for the Head Boy of Marton Grove School. I left England in 1963 for Canada and USA, but I kept-up on Cloughie's career. He certainly added a little Boro spice to the game, and the game is all the better for it. He may call himself 'Big 'Ead', but he wasn't really. Just full of confidence in his abilities. Why not a knighthood…he deserves one.' Joe Appleby, Lookout Mountain, Georgia, USA.

'I met Mr Clough when I was a young boy. I can remember how scared I was, but he was great. I still have the autograph. As a

Sunderland fan, I have come to admire his scoring achievements. I feel that he was the best England manager we never had. He should be knighted.' David Humphries.

'When he played for Sunderland, we all loved him – not only for his playing skills, but also for his outspoken comments to all and sundry. He has proved his class by overcoming horrendous injury, which stopped him from playing football, and showing everyone that he was also a class manager. Good luck in your efforts.' Joan Jones, Sunderland.

'I was born and bred in Middlesbrough and live a couple of minutes away from the street in which Cloughie lived. My grandad lived opposite him and I remember, as a child, my father recounting stories of him kicking a ball about in the street with Cloughie. He played for Boro and scored 200 goals at a rate of almost a goal a game (Cloughie that is, not my Dad).

'What would he cost in today's market? As a Boro fan I suppose it could be argued I might be slightly biased. But having read the other messages, it's obvious that he is respected and held in high regard not only in this country, but from far and wide. And rightly so. Arise, Sir Cloughie.' Paul Rose, Middlesbrough.

'If people are to receive recognition for services to the community, Brian Clough should receive a knighthood for all his work for the City of Nottingham and many charities, as well as what he did for the footballing communities of Derby and Nottingham Forest.' Andy Scott, Newark, Notts.

'My newspaper supports the campaign for Brian Clough to be knighted. When he came to Hartlepool United, the club I have supported since 1957, the whole town was buzzing. When we were promoted with the team Cloughie built and John McGovern, a Hartlepool lad, went on to lift the European Cup twice, the people of Hartlepool were proud. Arise, Sir Brian!' John Riddle, Sports Editor, *The Paper*, Tenerife, Canary Islands, Spain.

'Hey, he's got a great name. Every Englishman I meet comments on the skill, fame and legend of Mr Clough. Having followed his career as much as I could from "the wrong side of the pond", I can only imagine what a knighthood would mean to those who watched him and played for him, as well as the man himself.' Brian E. Clough, Walpole, Massachusetts, USA.

'A knighthood? Most definitely, yes. And those who denied him the England manager's job should be made to watch the ceremony – on their knees.' Ken Taylor, Manchester City fan.

'Brian Clough was one of football's greatest managers, not just in Britain but the world. He took mediocre teams and made them world beaters on a shoestring budget. Not only that but during a short playing career he was a prolific goalscorer. If Alex Ferguson was made Sir for his contributions to football then Cloughie should be Sir Brian also. He was and is a footballing legend. Simple as that.' Andrew Robinson, Cardiff.

'Not many "celebrities" have the effect of raising the hairs on the neck or bringing a huge lump to the throat. Brian Clough did that for thousands throughout his playing and managerial career, both by the simplicity of his tactics, his drive, charisma and sometimes his eccentricity. The sporting world has honoured one of its true greats – Sir Steve Redgrave. Without a doubt Brian Clough deserves to hold such a place in our hearts and be spoken of with the same deference as does Sir Steve.' Paul Bailey, Forest fan, Sutton-in-Ashfield, Notts.

'Brian Clough's teams gave millions of football fans around the world countless pleasure and fond memories of the game. He definitely deserves the title, "Sir". Thank you, Brian.' Lim Boon Cheng, Singapore.

'For the 125 members of Nottingham Forest Supporters Down Under, and the millions of Forest supporters throughout the world, Brian Clough represents for us the ultimate individual in football history. Many of us refer to Brian as "God". That is how important he is to us. I am sure I speak on behalf of every single Forest supporter in the world when I ask for Brian to be recognised in the general community of the Commonwealth, as we have done in the Nottingham Forest community for many years – a revered, treasured individual.' Todd Street, chairman of Nottingham Forest Supporters Down Under (Australian & New Zealand branch of official supporters club).

'I'm proud to add to the calls for Brian Clough to be knighted. I'll never forget the day I met him at an England Under-21 game. Though I am too young to have seen him play, fellow Sunderland fans who have rate him as one of the greats. As a manager, he was peerless. Unique, clever, entertaining. BC for KG!' Stephen Worthy, London.

'Here's another voice adding to the calls for the long overdue recognition. I was but a wee "young man" when I started supporting the Garibaldi Reds in the Eighties. Although I now reside in Australia, Cloughie is as much an icon for Forest supporters now than he ever was in his heyday. Knight him now!' Richard Wheatcroft, Australia.

'I would like to lend my voice to those calling for a knighthood for Brian Clough OBE. I am not, by any stretch of the imagination, a fan of Nottingham Forest or Derby County, but I consider that Mr Clough was a British hero of the last century. He was a man of principle and a man of action. He made a difference to many people's lives and gave his region, and indeed the country as a whole, reasons to be proud.' Ian Evans, London.

'I am an Englishman living in Australia. But word of such a worthy proposed knighthood travels fast and far. I have followed Forest for 30 years. There could never be a more worthy recipient of this award. It would be a truly great honour to a mountain of a man, and the best footballing brain our country has seen. Perhaps it would also replace some of Brian's regret at never being awarded the England manager's position. Hats off to Brian.' Andrew E. Dryden, Australia.

'If anyone deserves a knighthood for services to football, it has to be Brian. His goalscoring ability was uncanny. He was one of the greatest post war managers. Whatever ground he visits he always receives a standing ovation. We all at Middlesbrough love to see him when he comes home.' Mick Tucker, Northumberland.

'Cloughie did it 'the old fashioned way' and has earned a knighthood. Whether it was Hartlepool, Derby or Forest, he moulded a collection of character players and developed strong cohesive teams with limited finances. A true leader. Too bad the England national team bureaucrats never figured this out.' Bob Saveraux, Edmonton, Alberta, Canada.

'I'm sending this on behalf of my mother, who's 72 years of age and has lived in Nottingham all her life. She is not computer literate but took the trouble to write down the web address. She says "Knight Mr Clough. He deserves it a lot more than some of the b***ers who receive them." Excuse her French, but at 72 she expresses her views quite strongly these days. Please also add my vote, my husband's and daughter's. Brian Clough deserves a knighthood.' Helen Ledger, Newark, Notts.

'It is such a shame that this country has not officially recognised the outstanding contribution that Mr Clough has made to the national game. I strongly feel that he should be given a knighthood as public recognition for a truly unique man and his amazing achievements. Please, please, please don't let this be another person who is only ever talked about fondly by the establishment when he has passed away. Let him know now that his superb achievements and his wonderful philosophy and brand of football have been an inspiration to millions worldwide.' Glenn Haigh, York.

The Balcony Scene. Brian Clough and his wife Barbara on the balcony of Nottingham Council House during an end-of-season civic reception for Nottingham Forest in August 1989.

Photo courtesy of *Nottingham Post*.

Trophy Men. Nottingham Forest photographer John Sumpter is the other side of the lens, as he holds the Littlewoods Cup alongside Cloughie in the Master Manager's garden.

Our Match of the Day. Darren Nunn pictured with Cloughie on the day he proposed to his wife Sam at the City Ground. 'When I saw Brian, I became a gibbering wreck. Poor Sam had to calm me down,' says Darren.

'The best decision I ever made.' That's how Paul Hart describes his decision to sign for Brian Clough. Paul and his family are pictured with Cloughie in May 1983.

Photo courtesy of *Nottingham Post*.

A special moment. Former council leader Chris Williamson receives a hug and a kiss from his boyhood hero after a ceremony in which Cloughie was given the Freedom of Derby. 'It's the moment I treasure most about that day,' says Chris.

'Hey, you're a good-looking lad,' was Cloughie's complement to fan Richard Skelhorn at a book signing at Nottingham Forest. Recalls Richard: 'I'd just come back from holiday, so I think it was the sun tan that prompted that generous comment – I then went bright red! It was Brian's way of cracking a joke and making you feel relaxed. It was the only time I met him and I'll treasure those photos.'

Mission Accomplished. Jon Phipps made a 240-mile round trip to meet Cloughie in Burton-on-Trent. 'I'd read on the tribute website, brianclough.com, that he was signing books there – and I was determined to meet him,' says Jon. 'The photo is now proudly on my desk.'

'Brian had that special aura around him,' says former policeman Mike Hunter, who now lives in Florida. He's pictured with his son Ian alongside Cloughie.

The Young Man meets his hero. Author Marcus Alton with Cloughie at a fund-raising dinner in May 2001, for the Sir Stanley Matthews Foundation. 'Brian was the guest of honour that evening and was certainly the star of the show,' says Marcus. 'The audience hung on to his every word – before he ended the evening with "That's all for now. Go to bed." It was classic Clough.'

'I felt privileged to have known him,' recalls Colin Shields who is pictured presenting a bottle of champagne to Cloughie. 'Meeting Brian was a real life-changing experience for me. As a football fan, I began to have opportunities I could only have dreamt about.'

Cloughie has a kick-about with schoolchildren in Netherfield during a visit to officially open the town centre redevelopment work. Photo courtesy of *Nottingham Post*.

Happy Memories. Karl Egan is still proud of the photo he had taken with Cloughie when he was a little lad about 20 years ago. 'The photo shows that he never lost touch with supporters of all ages and they still think so much of him,' says Karl.

'It goes well in the bath.' That was Cloughie's comment to Marcus Alton and his wife Sarah when he presented them with a bottle of champagne for being the first in the queue at his very first book signing for *Walking on Water* in August 2002. Photo courtesy of *Nottingham Post*.

Back where it began. Cloughie is re-united with European Cup legend Kenny Burns at the City Ground during a visit in September 2003. 'He was like an adopted father to me,' reflects Kenny.

'I was his young lady for the day,' recalls Kay Hudson who accompanied Cloughie during a signing session at Nottingham Forest in 2002. 'I was both anxious and excited to meet Brian. He was warm, charming and quick witted. It was a very successful day and one I'll never forget,' says Kay.

An unforgettable day. Mike Simpson and his son Benjamin meet Cloughie at a book signing in Spondon, Derby. 'It was an honour to meet my hero,' says Mike.

Time to celebrate. 'Brian was on top form at a birthday party in Forest's Jubilee Club,' recalls Colin Shields who is pictured (right) with his brother Trevor.

Ship Ahoy! In this rare photo, Brian is pictured on a naval ship on a trip to the island of Gozo, during a visit to Malta. He was accompanied by Colin Shields who remembers: 'I turned to Brian and said: "This is fabulous, isn't it?" "Fabulous?" he replied, "I can't wait to get off this ship fast enough – I hate ships!"'

'I appreciated his friendship.' Former Nottingham Forest secretary Ken Smales receives a long-service award from Cloughie.

A piece of cake. Former Nottingham Forest secretary Ken Smales stands next to Brian and his wife Barbara as they prepare to cut a special Forest cake during a visit to a Staffordshire pottery.

Cloughie signs his name for fans during a visit to Burton Albion, where his son Nigel was manager, in April 2003. This was one of the first public photos of Brian following his liver transplant earlier that year.

Young fans have their books signed by Cloughie during a special appearance at a Nottingham book store in 2003. It was at this signing session that Brian thanked website editor Marcus Alton for passing on all the get well messages from fans following his liver transplant. 'To see so many people has been nothing short of incredible,' he told Marcus.

'Young man, he fits the bill.' Actor Colin Tarrant, who portrayed Cloughie in a tribute play, signs his name on a giant photo of the Great Man at Nottingham Playhouse following a gala performance. 'To have the opportunity to play my hero, Brian Clough, on stage was a dream come true,' says Colin, who is also pictured giving some advice – in typical Clough style – to European Cup legends John McGovern and Garry Birtles.

Never forgotten. Colin Shields holds one of the gifts he treasures from Brian. A tie, featuring a football symbol and the initials, BC. Only a few were made. 'I was very lucky to get one. Brian was really chuffed when we wore them,' says Colin.

TV presenter Gary Newbon interviews Barbara Clough at the unveiling of the superb bronze statue of Cloughie in Nottingham in November 2008. Gary says: 'I've interviewed many people during my career, but I put Brian Clough up there as the Number One.'
Photo courtesy of Neil Hoyle at www.hphoto.viewbook.com.

Cloughie legends (from left) Kenny Burns, Archie Gemmill and John McGovern join Gary Newbon on stage at the unveiling of the bronze statue of the Great Man in Nottingham.

Photo courtesy of Neil Hoyle at www.hphoto.viewbook.com.

Cloughie's captain John McGovern is interviewed by Gary Newbon during the unveiling ceremony for the bronze statue of the Master Manager in Nottingham.

Photo courtesy of Neil Hoyle at www.hphoto.viewbook.com.

Cloughie legend Martin O'Neill is interviewed by Marcus Alton on stage at the civic reception for Nottingham's bronze statue of Brian, held at the Council House in December 2008. Martin told Marcus: 'We would often disagree about my playing ability. I thought I was brilliant – but he didn't.'

Photo courtesy of Neil Hoyle at www.hphoto.viewbook.com.

Marcus interviews Cloughie legend John Robertson on stage at the civic reception for Nottingham's bronze statue of Brian, following a fund-raising campaign by fans. Recalled Robbo: 'He kept things simple and relaxation was important, especially before big matches.'

Photo courtesy of Neil Hoyle at www.hphoto.viewbook.com.

Cloughie legend Garry Birtles speaks to Marcus during the civic reception for the bronze statue of Brian in Nottingham. Said Garry: 'Life with the gaffer was so unpredictable – no two days were the same.'

Photo courtesy of Neil Hoyle at www.hphoto.viewbook.com.

A special souvenir. Former Nottingham Forest vice-chairman Jimmy Pell holds a replica of the European Cup made from Waterford glass. It was specially commissioned. 'Clough was a very generous man,' says Jimmy.

Colin Shields, Nottingham: 'Brian told me I had the most important job of the day – looking after his two sons.'

I was lucky enough to become one of the few people – besides the players – who Brian would allow to travel on the Nottingham Forest team coach. That all started after I was invited to the Forest team hotel before a match. My connections with Brian went back many years. I was originally a Derby supporter and became part of the campaign to have Brian re-instated at the Baseball Ground after he resigned. I was secretary of the supporters' club and we used to organise dances and fund-raising events to pay for the legal-side of things. At the same time, I was able to meet Brian and Barbara and all the players.

When Brian joined Forest, I bought a season ticket at the City Ground and another at Derby. My heart was at Derby, but it was being torn apart because of what I was seeing at Forest. Michael Keeling, who'd been a director at Derby and spearheaded the campaign to re-instate Brian, asked if I'd like to join them at a hotel in Leicester, where Forest were staying. I couldn't believe it. I was floating like a cloud. It was a fantastic opportunity for an ordinary supporter like me.

When I was at the hotel I was told that Brian wanted some Mannequins – the small cigars – and that I should take them up to his room. So I went up there and knocked on the door. Brian answered with a towel round him. 'I've brought these for you, Mr Clough,' I said. 'My name's Brian,' he replied. 'And I'll sort the money out with you when I come back down.' We all had lunch together before the match and then prepared to leave.

As the team was getting on the coach, Brian was at the hotel reception and a Leicester fan came up to him, pestering him. I said to the man, 'Would you mind not bothering Mr Clough, he's got a big job to do today. You'll have another opportunity some other time.' So he agreed and left him alone. Brian then turned round towards his support staff and said: ''Ere you lot, this man looks after me – he's my new minder.' And that stuck with me for quite a while. After the game, Brian got off the team coach and we took him back to his house in Quarndon.

It was unbelievable to think I was allowed on the Forest team coach. Not even the directors were allowed. It was my job to pick-up the newspapers and chocolates for the team, for when we were coming back. Sometimes I'd meet the coach at the Swallow Hotel on the A38, sometimes we'd drive to the away match in Brian's car. I would always add a few pork pies as well because I worked for Pork Farms. They used to tell me, 'Whilever they keep winning, you keep bringing those pies!' I continued to do that until Albert the driver told me not to bring any more. He said the players were just eating the meat and then chucking the pastry down the toilet. Admittedly, it was very rich pastry!

In the early days of those wonderful trips to Wembley, I was given the responsibility of looking after Brian's young sons, Simon and Nigel. Brian said to me, 'You've got the most important job of the day – looking after my two bairns.' I told him I was very proud to do it. After one of the games, I remember taking them round to the players' entrance and into the dressing room.

I also looked after one of Brian's VIP's. She was the widow of Harry Storer – the man who was essentially Brian and Peter Taylor's mentor. A lot of the things they did were in the style of Harry Storer. I would pick Mrs Storer up from Coventry and bring her to the match, and then take her back home again. I would take her into Brian's office and on one occasion she told him: 'This young man is wonderful, he looks after me so well.' Brian responded: 'Well, why do you think I sent him?'

Robert Nichols, from the Middlesbrough fanzine *Fly Me To The Moon*: 'The queue to see him snaked around the shopping centre.' I only ever met Brian Clough once in person but he left an impression. When he came to Middlesbrough to sign his autobiography it seemed everyone in town wanted to meet him. The queue snaked out of the bookshop and around the shopping centre, the sort of queue that you would usually only get for a pop star or A list celeb. But Brian was a celebrity and being from such a big family, everyone in Middlesbrough knew a Clough or had lived nearby. All wanted to trade anecdotes and Brian duly obliged.

Many years later I came to know Brian's elder brother Joe and sister Doreen as we met regularly in a group of fans, councillors and former football colleagues to plot our strategy for raising money for a statue of Brian in his hometown. It was a privilege to chat with the Clough family and eavesdrop on their memories of their brother when he was a 'young man.'

Of course, I also had my own family connections to the Cloughs. My mother had once dated another of Brian's brothers, Gerald, and I often wondered how life might have turned out for my brother and me if she had married into that great footballing family. Perhaps I wouldn't have been born with two left feet, or at least not the kind just reserved for standing on.

Every child of Middlesbrough is brought up on a tradition of our great centre-forwards. To Camsell, Fenton, Clough and

Hickton must now be added Slaven and Ravanelli. Great names passed on through families. But Cloughie's goalscoring heroics still leap off the page. How on earth did he manage to score at such an unbelievable rate? So close to a goal a game, it scarcely seems possible.

When the local paper the *Evening Gazette* announced the idea of building a statue, my Mam and me immediately came up with the plan that it should be the 'young man' walking through the park from his Valley Road house to the football ground, Ayresome Park. The man of the people in the people's park. Just as in that queue at the bookshop, he could be among friends, making a spectacle of himself for all time, stepping out ahead of the crowd.

Brian Clough, forever young-man.

Jason Taylor, Nottingham: 'We hung on his every word.'
My friend Hec Heathcote and I were lucky enough to meet Brian Clough and his managerial assistant Ronnie Fenton in a café bar in West Bridgford in Nottingham. It was after he had retired from management. We'd been to watch Forest's first game of the season against Sheffield Utd, and witnessed one of the best performances we'd mustered in recent years, a team resplendent with Michael

Dawson, Jermaine Jenas, Andy Reid et al. After enjoying this 'Brazil-like' spectacle at the City Ground, we retired to a café bar on Central Avenue.

We opened the door and walked up to the bar. As we did we both spotted Messrs Clough and Fenton sitting at a table. We smiled respectfully (in fact it was more shock and awe) and made our way over to the table next to the dynamic duo. The bar was practically empty, so we weren't sure whether we should sit as far away or as close as we dare. We chose the latter.

After a few minutes, Mr Clough, spotting we were Forest fans, beckoned us over to join him for a drink. We both shuffled over and pinched ourselves that this was really happening. Hec, being the son of Forest's club doctor of a few years back, Dr Heathcote, introduced us both — and that was it, we were in. Hec's Dad had helped Brian over the years and was well respected at the club. One thing about Brian is that if you were right by him, he would do anything for you.

We spent the next hour being regaled by brilliant stories of Brian's time in management, his 'qualifications' (his medals and Cups), his highs and his lows (falling out with Peter Taylor). He gave us his view on the new team that Paul Hart had assembled ('not bad, a good start from the young man') and his health ('just fine son, just fine').

As two life-long Forest fans, we sat in awe as our hero spoke. We hung on every word, and Mr Clough enjoyed having us as his audience. It was a match made in heaven, a memory we shall take to our grave. Thank you, Mr Clough.

Brent Gaunt, Gedling, Nottingham: 'The day I gave Mr Clough a lift.'

To this day, I still can't believe I gave Brian Clough a lift home. It was back in 2001 and I was following Arnold Town playing a Cup match against Burton Albion, where Brian's son Nigel was manager. We'd drawn 1–1 at Arnold's ground, and the replay was at Burton. We saw Brian walking to take his seat in the stand and didn't think we would get anywhere close to him. Arnold lost the match, and afterwards we saw Brian in the car park. I went over to shake his hand. I introduced him to my 14-year-old daughter, Helen, and my sister. My nephew had been playing for Arnold and was getting changed. Mr Clough said he'd enjoyed the match, and we stood talking for a while. He asked us where we lived, so I said we came from Nottingham.

Anyway, we ended-up giving him a lift back to Derby. I said I'd only got an Escort van, but he didn't mind. He got in the front and Helen was in the back. The car park was very busy, but everyone made way for us when they saw it was Mr Clough coming through. I kept calling him Mr Clough, but he said 'call me Brian.' I dropped him off, and he got a big wodge of money out of his pocket. I said I didn't want anything, but he insisted and gave £10 to Helen. 'You can buy some sweets,' he said. When I went to work, I told my workmates that I'd given Brian Clough a lift home and they didn't believe me at first. But they then realised it was true. It was a fantastic experience – and Helen has still got the £10 note.

Bernard Day, Middlesbrough: 'Sitting near Brian was quite an experience.'

I can honestly say that sitting near Brian Clough in the stand at Middlesbrough was quite an experience. This is how it came about. In the late Fifties I would watch Middlesbrough first team train on a regular basis – sometimes at Ayresome Park, sometimes at Hutton Road. The players would usually meet at Ayresome Park then run to Hutton Road. The main centre of my attention was the young Brian Clough. After training was over he would sign autographs for us youngsters. He could not be parted from Peter Taylor even in those days. It did not pay to listen into their conversation, let's just say there were always words we would not understand!

When Brian left Middlesbrough for Sunderland it came as a great shock. It was an even bigger shock when he was injured at such a tender age. I was on the Acklam Steel Works – Grove Hill bus going to his testimonial at Roker Park. It will give you some idea what Brian was like when, after the game, he insisted that the bus be held up until he could say thank you to all his family, neighbours and friends. Everyone was asking the same question: which club would he be coaching, or even managing, next? He just smiled and said nothing.

That club turned out to be Hartlepool, taking the then Burton manager Peter Taylor with him. We would always try to catch their games at every opportunity. When Brian moved on to Derby we had got into the habit of watching Hartlepool, the new manager was Gus McLean. He carried on Brian's tradition of driving the team bus to away games to save money. That's something I have never heard of before or since.

Some years later Brian was at Nottingham Forest and his right-hand man was Ron Fenton. They had to bring their side to

Ayresome Park on 22 April 1989. Unfortunately, a couple of weeks before that game Brian got into a bit of bother with the FA. Nottingham Forest fans ran onto the pitch at one of their home games. Brian was seen to belt one of his own fans right in front of the TV camera. He was banned from the bench.

Meanwhile, at Ayresome Park I always considered I had the best seat in the house (and in the best company with Ted Briam, now aged 88). You can imagine our surprise when Brian Clough came up and sat two seats away! Brian pointed out that he got a little excited during matches and made apologies to us all before things got out of hand. He didn't let us down!

When Forest got a corner at one end of the ground, Brian started to tell Fenton he thought his goalkeeper, Steve Sutton, was not concentrating at the other! Screaming, let's say, words of encouragement. Some youngsters had turned their heads to look at Brian. He then started to tell them that he used to work for Middlesbrough. I honestly don't think that the kids knew who he was – they were looking at him because he was screaming at the players so much. In the second half, Brian decided that one of his midfield players was venturing into Middlesbrough's half of the field. 'How many times do we have to tell him not to cross the halfway line? He's already done it twice.' Brian starts screaming, 'Get back.' The player looks over to Brian and just stares.

Me and Ted could not watch the best match of the season and watch Brian at the same time. Forest were at their best with precision passing and superb team work. Middlesbrough took the lead through Ripley. Forest made it 1–4 before Slaven and Davenport made the score more flattering for Middlesbrough, 3–4. You would think Brian would be a happy man. No, he was watching for the first signs of Nottingham Forest players easing up! Gaynor looks over but ignores his manager: Gaynor off, Chettle on! Brian was sitting over the tunnel. He shouts to Gaynor, 'Make the tea! I want two sugars in mine please.' This was followed by a howl of his own laughter. Honestly, you should have seen Gaynor's face – if looks could kill! I wondered what might have happened if Middlesbrough were winning.

Yes, there's no doubt that sitting near Brian Clough was quite an experience!

Kenneth Clarke MP: 'Brian's problem with a work permit.'

Brian Clough would occasionally approach me when he needed assistance in getting a work permit or visa for an overseas player.

For a time in the late 1980s I was a Minister at the Department of Employment with some overall responsibility for work permits, when Brian Clough complained to me about the refusal of a permit for a Swedish player he had signed, in the years when work permits were still required for Swedes.

The application had been dealt with by a Miss Smith, on her first day at her desk in that division. She had sent him a standard letter refusing a work permit in the absence of evidence that no suitable unemployed British citizen was available to fill the post. The letter told Brian Clough that the best evidence would be produced if he advertised the vacant midfield position in the local newspaper at least three times and could prove that no suitable applicant was available.

I will leave Brian's telephone expression of his views on the subject of having to offer this key role to someone from the local dole queue to the readers' imagination! The player he was trying to sign was an established Swedish international recruited after Brian had failed to get Glenn Hoddle, who had gone to Italy instead. This did comply with the rules for professional footballers. The work permit was granted, and some unfortunate unemployed lad in Nottingham was deprived of the opportunity of having a go at a midfield role in one of the best football clubs in England at that time!

Ray Mallon, Mayor of Middlesbrough: 'He had incredible charisma, but there was a humble side to him too.'

As a young lad, I followed Brian Clough's career very closely, and I went to his testimonial game at Sunderland in October 1965. He was a great footballer who oozed confidence and had incredible charisma both on the field and off it.

His achievements for Middlesbrough Football Club are the stuff of legend and it's not hard to see why he is still held in such great affection. From his childhood home in Valley Road, he would walk through Albert Park to the former Ayresome Park for Boro's home games.

The striking statue of Brian in the park, with his boots slung over his shoulder, is a permanent and fitting reminder of the heights achieved by an ordinary – well, far from ordinary in fact – Boro lad.

Although he was a great footballer, I think he was an even greater manager with an astonishing record that speaks for itself. But he also had a humble side. When he was manager of Hartlepool, I recall a young lad of about 10 getting hit in the face by the ball when it was kicked out of play during a game. He went over and got the kid and sat with him throughout the rest of the match, which is a mark of the man. He was a legend, pure and simple.

John Sumpter, Nottingham Forest photographer: 'I felt a tug on my sleeve, and Cloughie pulled me through the crowd of people.' After the League Cup Final in 1989, Cloughie invited me onto the Forest team coach and I ended-up with the trophy on my knee! I'd travelled down to Wembley on the bus organised by the club's Commercial Office. After the game, in which Forest beat Luton Town, I was in the dressing room, where the champagne was flowing. Cloughie turned to me and asked: 'How did you get down here today?' I told him I'd travelled on the commercial office coach. 'Well, you can come back with us!' he replied. I couldn't believe it – it was like a dream come true for a Forest fan like me to travel on the team bus.

On the coach, I sat just behind Cloughie and alongside the journalist, John Lawson. I remember the motorway was heaving with traffic as we made our way home and the Cup was passed around – at one point I was lucky enough to hold the trophy in my lap! I didn't realise you had to keep quiet if you sat near Cloughie and I was just chatting away, excited by this unique opportunity. Then Cloughie turned round and said: 'If I hear your voice one more time…' I didn't want to be thrown off the coach, so I asked if I could go to the back of the bus to take some photographs of the players with the trophy. Cloughie agreed, so I went behind the curtain which separated the two halves of the coach and took some photos – and had a bit more to drink to join-in with the celebrations. But I soon felt my head spinning with all the drink and eventually had to rest my head on one of the tables. The coach stopped at East Midlands Airport, where Cloughie had arranged to get a lift home.

On the following Tuesday, Forest were playing Southampton at the City Ground. When Cloughie saw me he remembered what had happened and said: 'You were an absolute disgrace on that coach – I'm not letting you do that again!' Nevertheless, I had some fantastic times working with Brian. He was always co-operative when I needed a photograph. I think he liked being told what to do when we were lining-up a photo. He wasn't keen on 'Yes Men' – he liked people to stand up to him and show they weren't afraid of him.

But the first time I went into his office, I just stood there, like a schoolboy in the Headmaster's study. He said: 'Don't stand there, sit down.' He wanted to make sure I was relaxed. He had great charisma, and it was a huge privilege to work with him. Once you got to know him, the fear factor disappeared. The very first team photo I took was in September 1978. From then onwards, I was lucky enough to capture some special moments during the height of all the success.

After the European Cup Final victory over Hamburg in Madrid, the players took the trophy into a corner of the stadium and I managed to get a photo of them, even though the officials turned the floodlights off! I was also fortunate to get into the dressing room – thanks to Cloughie. There were lots of security officials in the tunnel, and Peter Taylor was trying to negotiate my way through them. But Cloughie got fed-up with the delay. All of a sudden, I felt a tug on my sleeve and Cloughie pulled me through the crowd of people. I got into the dressing room and took photographs of the team with the trophy.

One very special moment for me came when I was taking some family photographs in Cloughie's back garden. I had the opportunity of having a photo of me with Brian and two of

Forest's trophies – the Littlewoods Cup and the Zenith Data Systems Trophy. I'd set-up the camera on a tripod and Brian's son Simon did the honours and took the picture for me. It's one I still treasure – Cloughie signed it: 'John, lots of love, Brian.' The photo is now framed as a special memory of a remarkable man.

Steven Fletcher, *Nottingham Post* newspaper: 'The day I secured a special interview with Cloughie.'

I remember the only time I interviewed Brian Clough. I was slightly hungover one Saturday, the Easter of the year Cloughie had his liver transplant. We'd carried thousands of good luck messages for him in the paper, but had never had an interview.

I walked into his son's shop, and there he was. I thought: 'Crikey, we've not had an interview since his op.' So I went outside, and rang the newsdesk, to ask them to send me a photographer, paper and pen. They did, and in the meantime Cloughie had gone into the back of the shop. I asked his son Simon if he would speak to me and got a 'yes'.

Our photographer arrived, and eventually Cloughie came out. He was slow and frail, but he walked up to me, looked me up and down and said: 'Six foot six, central defender.' I said 'Yes sir, but not a very good one!' and then we did the interview. He was utterly charming, said a lot of nice things about Paul Hart's Play-off contenders and said he would pose for a picture if I mentioned his son's shop (never shy of publicity!). I went into work, and we splashed it on the front page of our next edition.

Karl Egan, Derbyshire: 'I still treasure my photo with Cloughie.'
I'm still proud of the photograph I had taken with Cloughie when I was just a toddler. Brian Clough is a personal hero of mine, not least because he achieved unthinkable things with Nottingham Forest and came out with some cracking quotes! I am now a 21-year-old student at university in Nottingham. I'm from South Normanton in Derbyshire and have been a lifelong Forest fan. The picture was taken at the City Ground behind the Executive/Brian Clough Stand, where Cloughie had gone out to meet the fans. There was apparently a large queue, but he had photos taken with all the supporters and signed autographs.

I'm not sure exactly how old I was, but I'd have a guess at one or two years of age, so it would have been 1991/1992. My Dad took the picture as he used to take me to a lot of games even when I was too young to remember. But I think in this case it was an event at the end of the season, rather than a match. Although I can't remember it being taken, the photo is something I treasure, because Brian Clough was a tremendous figurehead of Nottingham Forest. The photo shows that he never lost touch with the supporters, who still think so much of him. I've now had the photograph framed – after all, not a lot of people have a photo of themselves with Forest's greatest manager!

Roy McFarland, who won the First Division Championship with Cloughie at Derby County: 'We all listened to Brian – and invariably he was right.'

From the first day I met him, I certainly knew things were going to happen at Derby County. And they did happen. Yes, it took 12 months for us to kick-off and get things going. I think with the signing of Dave Mackay and after that Willie Carlin, all of a sudden we had a team that sailed out of the Second Division and obviously did very, very well in the First Division.

They were fantastic times. It was a great period in my football career. They were the best six years I had in football. We all listened to what Brian said – and invariably he was right. At times, it could be a little bit annoying because he would antagonise the opposition sometimes, especially the likes of Mr Revie and Leeds United. But when Brian said things to you, you knew what he'd seen and what he was talking about was spot-on.

The minute I signed for him, he drew an unbelievable picture of what would happen with my career. I had absolutely no idea that what he was saying would happen – and it did happen for me. I did play for England, we did have success, we did eventually win the First Division Championship and we did qualify for Europe. These were things we'd never have dreamed about.

David Brewster, Nottingham: 'The League Cup was standing proudly on the shop counter.'

I met Brian not long after Nottingham Forest won the League Cup for the first time, back in 1978. It was the Sunday after they'd beaten Liverpool in the replayed Final at Old Trafford. I went into the Post Office at Bramcote, which was run by Brian's brother, and Brian was behind the counter. And on top of the counter was the League Cup!

I was with my son Gary, who was 11 or 12 at the time, and Brian told him to put the Cup in the shop window. 'Make sure it's right at the front,' he said. So Gary carefully placed the trophy in the window and put it proudly on show. It's something I'll never forget.

Pauline Davies, Nottingham: 'Brian asked my grandson to take a penalty.'

It was back in the Eighties when my husband took my grandson Alex to watch Nottingham Forest training. Alex was about eight years old at the time. The players were taking penalties and all of a sudden Cloughie turned to Alex and said: 'Come on, show them how it's done.' So Alex took a penalty and scored! Brian also invited them into the Forest trophy room. Alex will never forget that day.

'Dickiebo' writer and blogger: 'The dinner date that caused a problem.'

I met Cloughie one day at Cardiff Arms Park, the famous rugby ground. Clive Thomas, the top referee, worked for the same firm as me and wrote a book *Why Me* – and Cloughie came to Cardiff for the launch. Well, that took all afternoon and Clive and Cloughie were due to travel on to Barry, some half-hour's ride away, to attend a 'boys club' dinner with Clive's mate, Frankie Vaughan, the singer. Clive was trying to hurry Cloughie, as they were going to be late. But Cloughie refused absolutely to go, unless Clive would guarantee me a place at their top-table! In a nutshell, it was a top fund-raising dinner, fully sold-out. That was stalemate, Clive pleading that nothing could be done, Cloughie saying 'If Dick doesn't come, then I'm not going!' Clive was frantically looking at his watch, begging. Cloughie was not moving. How was it settled? Well, I had to 'walk-out' on them. A pity, 'cos as you've perhaps guessed, I liked Cloughie and really got on with him. The man died far too young, and an awful lot of us miss him. Not many people do you meet just the once and have such memories of, but Cloughie – for me – was one.

Martin Kerry: 'The day I met Cloughie at the airport.'
I can't remember the exact date this happened, but it was at a book signing at East Midlands Airport not long before the news of Cloughie's liver transplant hit the papers. The scenario: a life-long supporter of Nottingham Forest awaits a genius…

Given the rumours already circulating about his health, I was surprised by his vigorous arrival as he strode past the long queue outside a book shop, accompanied by his son Nigel. As the queue moved forward and I came within earshot of the desk piled high with books set up for him outside the store, I heard him engage genuinely with every person who stood in front of him.

An old lady in her late seventies was the last before me, and the conversation went something like this:

BC: 'Hello my darling, and what's your name.'

OL: 'I'm Ethel, and I've been waiting 30 years to meet you.'

BC: 'Well you've met me now. Tell me Ethel, are you an old-age pensioner like me?'

OL: 'Yes I am.'

(From this point his voice rose steadily in the way it must have done when giving an errant player a good telling off.)

BC: 'Well you shouldn't have come here today love.'

OL: 'Oh, why ever not?'

BC: 'You should have come to the one I did at ASDA in West Bridgford last week. It was £3 off there. THEY DON'T CHARGE FULL PRICE LIKE THESE ROBBING B******S!'

By the end, you could have heard him from Terminal Two, if they'd got one, and the manageress standing behind him in her best uniform was looking desperately for a hole to dive into.

Then it was my turn. Immediately, he clocked my cricket jersey and asked me about my club. After some cricket chat, he signed my book, and I asked him 'Can I be cheeky daft and ask you to sign another one?'

'Of course.' he said, reaching for the pile.

Me: 'No, this one'

BC: 'OK, what's that then?'

Me: 'Lawson's *History of Nottingham Forest*, signed by him and the whole of the Championship squad. My Mam used to work with Garry Birtles' Mam, and he got me the lot, but you were on holiday.'

Brian opened the book, looked at the first page, shook his head and said 'Weren't many of them, were there?' For there were only 15 signatures. I concurred.

BC: 'Where would you like me to sign?'

Me: 'Any where you bloomin' well like.'

He popped his signature smack in the centre of the inside cover.

To meet Cloughie that day was something that I would not have missed for the world. As I drove away from the airport I remember thinking, if someone can make somewhere like an airport concourse a better place just by being there, then they really must be a bit special.

Lee Allsop, Nottingham: 'I kissed him on both cheeks.'

At the end of the 1992–93 season when Forest went down and Cloughie resigned, 'Cloughie's last Forest match' seemed to be forever being put forward (such as Sheff United at home, then

Ipswich away, then Forest/Notts in the County Cup Final etc). Finally, it seemed to settle on Forest reserves v Stoke reserves at home in midweek. I went and sat in the Main Stand.

Somehow, after the match I found myself somewhere underneath the directors' box or near the tunnel or somewhere, I've never been sure (not my stand and I was drunk at the time). There was a bunch of other fans there, of whom I was at the front. Then from a door at the side Brian Clough appeared accompanied by Paul White, the club secretary. He looked a bit shaky and they both stood there, as though wondering what we were going to do. I went up and shook his hand. I said 'thanks Brian' then hugged him and gave him a big kiss on both cheeks. A few other lads said 'thanks Brian'.

I stepped back and he pointed his finger at us all, shaking a bit. Then he said, 'BE GOOD!' He went inside and we all went home. Looking back, I don't think I ever really believed I would meet Brian Clough anywhere close-up to thank him personally for all the great times. It never entered my head that I would get the chance. However, since that meeting, and especially since Brian died, I have always been glad that when the opportunity arose I acted the way I did.

Brian Tansley, journalist and broadcaster: 'He was never too far away from displaying a soft centre – as we found out that morning.'

Talk about being thrown in at the deep end! It was late 1979, and I had been offered the role of Sports Editor at Radio Trent, following in the illustrious footsteps of Clive Tyldesley and Andy Smith.

I was already covering Notts County's matches at home and away on a freelance basis, but this offer was something completely different – as they say. Only after agreeing terms did I stop to think that if Jimmy Sirrel was a nightmare to handle at Meadow Lane, then the prospect of dealing with Brian Clough and Peter Taylor on a regular basis was even more daunting. I was soon to find out that there was an extra element which needed addressing.

Listeners from the era will remember that we had one of the first football phone-in shows for an hour on Saturday evenings, hosted by a certain Chris Ashley. Chris revelled in the moniker of 'The Mouth of the Midlands' for his outrageous presentation style. He wasn't everybody's cup of tea on-air, but he was certainly compulsive listening – and off-air a really nice guy for whom I have a lot of time and admiration.

Unbeknown to me, Chris's style – and certain comments – had resulted in Radio Trent being barred from covering matches at the City Ground on more than one occasion, and the general bonhomie between the European champions and the radio station were pretty fraught to say the least.

Word came back to me that Messrs Clough and Taylor were particularly unhappy at being labelled 'Bill and Ben'. Well who wouldn't be – outside of two little men made out of flowerpots who lived behind a potting shed at the bottom of a suburban garden! But I digress.

After a few days of getting no joy at all from my attempts to speak to one or other of the pair, I was pleasantly surprised to be granted an audience with them one morning to talk things over and assure them that we would rein Mr Ashley back if he continued to overstep the mark. With more than a glint of mischief in his eyes, Chris asked me whether I'd like him to join me on the mission – and it might be my imagination, but I'll swear he grimaced a little when I agreed.

Having arrived at the City Ground, we were shown into a large room, which it transpired was Peter Taylor's office. Peter arrived, we shook hands, and he was as pleasant and welcoming as you could wish. So far so good, I thought.

Suddenly, from down the corridor, bellowed a familiar tone. 'I recognise that ******** voice. What's that maniac doing in my football club?' And in strode Brian Clough. In his pomp Cloughie was as sharp as a tack. Mischievous and overwhelming, time taught you that he was never too far away from displaying a soft centre – as we were to find out that morning.

Peter played his part in defusing the situation and within 10 minutes we were treated to some hilarious stories from the pair over a cup of coffee. The outcome was that I think they appreciated us going into the lion's den, so to speak, and Mr Ashley promised that he wouldn't call them Bill and Ben on-air any longer.

Come the weekend I was driving towards Meadow Lane ready to report on Notts County's latest match when I switched on the radio to hear what the new supposedly squeaky-clean Mouth of the Midlands had to say. It was the era when we didn't have to do a preview until around a quarter to three, so I had the luxury of arriving a little later than reporters and commentators have to these days. We had left the City Ground on such good terms that I was far from prepared for what I heard next.

'RIGHT!' roared the familiar voice over the airwaves. 'What's the Ayatollah and his mate been up to this week?'

It's the closest I've ever come to driving up the curb and ploughing into a queue of innocents at a bus stop. The afternoon passed in a blur and the Mouth was back in abrasive mode having digs at all and sundry. It just proved to me that with the best will in the world some things will never change.

I think Brian and Peter accepted that – plus the fact that they had more important things on their mind like retaining the European Cup, rather than taking the bait from a very clever media man.

Phil Burrows: 'The most memorable time of our lives.'

One cold winter's night, my son and daughter Louis and Kayleigh were mascots at Burton Albion FC. As their photographs had been published in the match-day programme, we decided to collect some autographs. The next thing I heard was, 'Hey Phil, Cloughie's in here, ask him.' I approached Brian for his autograph; what an experience.

He signed obligingly and then spent 30 minutes talking to my children about life, behaviour and football until we had to apologise to him for leaving to go outside and watch the football match. What a truly magnificent ambassador for the game of football. It was the most memorable 30 minutes of my family's life.

Sam Allardyce, West Ham boss and former Notts County, Bolton and Blackburn manager: 'My tribute to Brian.'

Sadly, I never got to spend enough time in Brian's company to be able to add to the many tales that have become football folklore. Brian Clough changed the face of football in this country, and his contribution in bringing the game to a wider audience cannot be overlooked.

He bestrode the game like a Colossus, and football is a much richer place for having had him in it. He may have been outspoken, but that he backed up his words with solid technical nous cannot be denied. The fact his name is still talked about in football is a testament to his impact upon it.

Julie Heseltine, Nottingham: 'We were granted an audience with our hero.'

Many years ago when we were children, we used to wait in the City Ground car park for the team to arrive for training – and hopefully add to the many autographs we already had in our Forest autograph book. On this particular Friday morning, Brian Clough arrived and I asked him politely for his autograph…only 'please' would be acceptable you see.

'Come with me,' Mr Clough said to me and my younger sister, Susan. We followed him through the main reception doors, turned right and down the corridor, to be taken into his office and asked to sit down in front of his desk. 'Danger – dynamic boss' greeted me from a plaque on his desk. The office was full of red-and-white teddies, and on the side wall was the first-team list and reserves list alongside it. 'What is your name?' he asked. 'Susan,' my sister replied. He wrote: 'To Susan, Be Good, Brian Clough.' He turned to me. 'What is your name?' 'Julie,' I replied. 'To Julie, Be Good, Brian Clough.' Our autograph books were now complete.

'My son, Nigel, will show you the way out…' Mr Clough finished our audience with him and we returned to the car park with our Mum, totally shocked by what had just happened and with many envious supporters standing…watching…wondering…

Mr Brian Clough was a one-off, and speaking as a loyal Nottingham Forest supporter, come rain or shine, Championship or Premiership – this memory will stay with me forever. Thank you, Mr Clough for giving me some fabulous times as a supporter – and as I sit in the Trent End and see your name at the top of your stand, my memories can never be forgotten.

John Preston, Los Altos, California, United States: 'My surprising conversation with Brian.'

I was born in Thornaby near Middlesbrough in 1942. At the age of 17, in 1959, I was playing for Billingham Synthonia Juniors and had an opportunity to meet Brian Clough at a Youth Club meeting on Fairfield Estate.

It was an interesting and very ironic discussion. Brian at the time was very much the local hero and full of confidence and ego. The ironic part of the discussion was when I asked him: 'Mr Clough, what do you most dislike about the game?'

He answered: 'There are too many restrictions put upon a player in his contract with management and club. I cannot ride a motorbike, as an example. The thing I most dislike about the game and would never consider pursuing is the role of manager! They are the most [expletives deleted] reprehensible and despicable part of the game!'

It's ironic that after a career cut short far too early, he should become and set the standard for those 'reprehensible and despicable' managers.

He was a true Yorkshireman, blunt and honest and always striving to be the best. On the few occasions when I was able to watch a game, I was always impressed with his ball distribution and his ability to stand next to the centre-half, pivot and score a goal in the 89th minute.

Day, Maclean, Clough, Peacock and Holliday. How we would love to have that line back. God watch out, Brian might just want your job.

Muhammad Dinath, Pretoria, South Africa: 'He will never be forgotten.'

It's a pity that I was born in an era after Clough's heroics. I would have loved to watch him as a player and manager. By no means am I a Middlesbrough, Derby, Forest or Leeds fan. Rather I'm a Manchester United fan, who appreciates great football and footballing legends, and Mr Clough is certainly right up there. Salute to a legend who will never be forgotten in true footballing fans' hearts.

Jimmy Pell, former Nottingham Forest vice-chairman: 'We celebrated winning the European Cup by eating beef burgers.'

We had some wonderful times, and the European trips in particular were great fun. Before the first European Cup Final in Munich in

1979, we stayed in a lovely hotel in nearby Augsburg. It was a beautiful place. I remember we took a trip down to the town square. There was a cyclist there who was from Nottingham, and he fell off his bike when he saw Clough. He couldn't believe it. So Brian decided to help him out and arranged for him to camp in the grounds of the hotel!

When Clough went to see his team the night before the European Cup Final, he took them a case of champagne. He told them they might as well drink it because otherwise they wouldn't be able to get to sleep.

Clough had given all the chefs at the Augsburg hotel tickets to go to the European Cup Final. So when we won and got back to the hotel, they made us beef burgers to celebrate and we had the European Cup on the table.

Clough moulded the players into a marvellous team and he managed the club in the right way. We'll never see his like again.

Justin Heaton, East Midlands: 'Brian was eating a cup of mushy peas.'

My earliest memory of Brian Clough was when he came to watch his son Nigel playing for my local team, Heanor Town. I remember everyone whispering about him being there and I don't think anyone actually said anything to him. I think he was with his assistant Ronnie Fenton. The only recollection I have from this is that he was sitting with his legs over the seats in front, eating a cup of mushy peas. It must have been around 1984 — and not long after that, Nigel was playing regularly for him at Forest.

For anyone that tried to get his autograph while he was Forest manager, they will know he didn't just stand around signing, but basically got out of his white Mercedes and walked through the main City Ground entrance doors. The doorman then instructed about 5–10 people to line up at the door and they were then let inside. You then had to line up in a corridor outside the office and were ushered in, a couple at a time. Once inside the manager's office you were faced with the great man who sat in his chair behind his desk and signed your autograph book. 'Be Good Justin, Brian Clough' he wrote for me. I think when I went in, Ronnie Fenton was sitting in the corner. I remember by the time you actually got in the office you were pretty nervous, and as I was only about 15 at the time I didn't actually say anything to him.

I also remember seeing him on a football field somewhere in Derby when my brother was playing for the local boys team. There were two pitches together, and Brian's eldest son Simon was playing on the other pitch. Nobody really approached him until the kids' match had finished. Then once someone had broken the ice he was surrounded by autograph hunters. He didn't mind and was happily signing footballs and anything else that people put in front of him.

I went to a reserve match at the City Ground in the 1980s and saw that Brian was sitting in the Directors' Box, so I said to my brother 'When he gets up, we'll try and catch him on his way to the car for an autograph.' Midway through the game he suddenly appeared in the stand and ordered about four youths to get up out of their seats. He then marched them out of the ground, so me and my brother got up and followed. I remember standing at the top of the steps at the back of the Main Stand watching Brian shouting at these youths from where the souvenir shop is now and basically making sure they had left the ground. Because he was so angry we decided not to approach him for an autograph that night!

My lasting memory of Brian is the rain-soaked night at Pride Park for his memorial service. I think it was Nigel that said 'I bet he's looking down on us saying look at those idiots sat in the rain' or words to that effect. He will always have a lasting effect on me – for example, how to play the game right: 'football wasn't meant to be played in the clouds etc' and 'get your hair cut and have a shave young man.' These are things that I will instill into the boys team that I run — and ideals that I will take to my grave.

Colin Shields, Nottingham: 'I still treasure the tie Brian gave me.'
Brian was a very generous man. I used to visit him at his house. We both loved Frank Sinatra — I still do. On one occasion he gave me a framed photo of Ol' Blue Eyes. But more than that, he took us all to the Albert Hall in London to see Sinatra perform — we had the best seats in the house. I sat alongside Sir Bobby Robson. Sinatra even mentioned Brian during the concert.

I remember the show was Sinatra, Sammy Davis Junior and Liza Minnelli. Brian had already been down there to see the show, but this time he took a bus load of people. It must have cost him a fortune. I wanted to pay my own way and I went down to the City Ground and made sure I paid him back. 'Thanks very much,' he said. 'You're the only one who's paid me.'

His generosity was also demonstrated when we used to return from away matches. When we were leaving the ground, the team coach would get a police escort away from the stadium. At a suitable point, Brian would arrange for the police outriders to be given a tip, something like £50. Then the boss of the outriders would climb aboard the coach and say: 'Thank you very much, Mr Clough.' He would reply: 'Hey, thanks a lot for what you're doing, too.'

One of the gifts I treasure is a tie that Brian gave me. Only a few were made, and they had a football symbol on them with his initials, BC. I was very lucky to get one. Brian was really chuffed when we wore them.

I remember Brian was on top form at a birthday party for one of my relatives. We held the party in the Jubilee Club at Forest's City Ground, and I still have the photo of him standing alongside my brother Trevor and me. On another occasion I was fortunate enough to present him with a big bottle of champagne to celebrate yet another of his many managerial achievements. Again, the photo of that moment remains very special.

Meeting Brian was a real life-changing experience for me. As I got to know him, he had such a major effect. I became more confident, especially when dealing with people. As a football fan, I began to have opportunities I could only have dreamt about. It was a wonderful experience, a wonderful journey. He was a very caring man, and he loved his family. I felt very privileged to have known him.

Rich Fisher, Nottingham: 'I invited Cloughie to my birthday party.'

I have always been brought up to believe in the old saying 'If you don't ask, you don't get'. Of course, I've learned over the years that the saying isn't always true. However, one person who made it true for me as a young lad back in the early 1990s was none other than my hero!

That hero was Brian Clough. Back in those days, Cloughie was still in his pomp at the City Ground – and like most Forest fans, I idolised him. Even at a young age, I knew that our manager was somehow a whole lot more special than the others – the way he talked, his idiosyncratic behaviour…and most importantly of course, the way his football teams always played.

My admiration for him was without bounds. Or so I thought! Somehow, my respect for the great man increased even further following a little incident that occurred around my 12th birthday.

As is the way when you reach that sort of milestone, my parents said I could have a birthday party – and that I could invite my friends. And I did. But I also invited an extra guest – yes, Cloughie!

Looking back, it's crazy to think that I ever thought a busy football manager with a family of his own was ever going to come to a birthday party being thrown by a young lad who he'd never met, and join in with a kick-about in the back garden or whatever my pals and I were planning to get up to. Of course, though, young minds aren't blessed with such logic – and as I sat down and wrote him a polite letter of invite (remembering of course to address him as 'Mr Clough'), I actually believed that there might be half a chance that he'd turn up.

Come the big day, I found myself running to the window in the front room every time I heard a car pull up – half hoping it would be Cloughie! Of course, he never came – and while my birthday party was fantastic nonetheless, I couldn't help but feel a tinge of disappointment when it got to the end of the day and there'd been no sign of my hero.

A few days later though, something incredible happened – a package came through the post. Now getting ANYTHING through the post is exciting when you're a kid – but a large package? With a NOTTINGHAM FOREST postmark on it?

I tore the package open – and unbelievably, it was a letter from Cloughie himself, wishing me a happy birthday and apologising for not having been able to make it to my party. What's more, he'd also enclosed a football signed by himself and the entire Forest squad!

Needless to say, I was walking on air for the rest of the week – and to this day, the football remains a cherished possession...

Richard Skelhorn, Nottingham: 'He told me I was a good looking lad – it must have been the sun tan!'

I'll never forget my one and only encounter with the Great Man. Although I'd seen him hundreds of times at the City Ground, not to mention at away grounds and at Wembley, since attending my first Forest match as a young boy, I'd never actually met Old Big 'Ead.

A book-signing at the Forest merchandise shop to mark the publication of Brian's autobiography *Walking on Water* gave me the opportunity I'd longed for. I'd heard about the book-signing while on holiday abroad in the summer of 2002. It was due to take place on the day I came home and so it was on the return flight that I made the decision to go along.

I arrived at the City Ground nice and early and, to my surprise, found myself reasonably close to the front of the queue. I recall chatting to the young chap standing behind me, who introduced himself as Rich. Much later I realised he was Rich Fisher, who was part of the campaign to raise funds for the Brian Clough statue in

Nottingham city centre. Anyway, the doors to the club shop opened and as the waiting fans poured inside, I stood a mere few feet away from the man who I'd revered all my life.

I couldn't help noticing how much Brian had aged since those Saturday afternoons spent watching him in the dugout and on the touchline at the City Ground wearing his distinctive green sweatshirt, barking out orders to the men in the Garibaldi shirts. But, listening to him chat to those having their books autographed, I realised that despite his earlier health problems he'd lost none of his quick wit and trademark mannerisms – such as the finger-wagging and addressing us blokes as 'young man.'

Sat next to him was his trusty assistant, Ron Fenton, who I'd also seen hundreds of times at Forest matches. I remember feeling quite touched that he'd remained loyal to Brian long after his legendary managerial career came to an end and was still, quite literally, by his side.

My abiding memory is not from my own encounter with Brian, but from his television interview with former *Central News* sports reporter Keith Daniell a few minutes before I was due to have my book signed.

I recall the reporter asking Brian something along the lines of 'Is it always more special coming back to the City Ground than Derby?' I really hoped Brian would say 'Yes, of course – I enjoyed my greatest triumphs at Forest,' or something similar – even if he'd only be saying it to please the waiting Forest fans and tell them what they wanted to hear.

But deep down I knew he'd never publicly declare a greater affection for one set of fans over the other. So, while Brian wasn't usually known for his diplomacy – the opposite in fact! – I wasn't at all surprised when he replied that he had huge affection for both clubs and couldn't possibly choose between the two.

However, that hasn't stopped me replaying the scene over in my head countless times – but this time with Brian uttering the line I so desperately longed for!

My actual encounter with Clough was brief, but I won't ever forget it. When it came to my turn to have my book signed, I asked Brian if I could have my photograph taken with him. Naturally he was only too happy to oblige. As I sat down next to him he quipped that I was a good-looking lad, which made me go bright red! But I guess it was just Brian's way of cracking a joke and making me feel relaxed. It must have been my sun-tan (not to mention the fact I was a lot younger back then) that spurred this particularly generous comment!

I'd handed Rich Fisher my camera and asked him if he'd take a few snaps while I chatted to Brian. He duly did the honours, and

I'll treasure those photos, along with my signed book featuring Brian's trademark 'Be Good' instruction, forever.

The thing I remember most about Brian was his warmth and the genuine interest he showed in everyone who turned out to see him. While the prospect of meeting Brian could be daunting, and even intimidating, he would quickly say something to make you laugh which immediately put you at ease.

My brief encounter with the Great Man will live long in my memory, just like everything he did for my beloved Forest.

Roy Mullin, Nottingham: 'I was so awestruck, I forgot to ask for his autograph.'

I was fortunate enough to meet Brian Clough in the early Eighties, through my sister. She and a friend met Brian one night at a Duncan Norvelle event at a club. Brian invited my sister to come along to a game against Leicester City. He gave her two free tickets which also included free parking in the guest area. Luckily, my sister took me along too.

I was amazed when we were invited into his office on the day of the match. It was surreal as I could hear the crowd chanting outside and — there was me and my sister, chatting to Brian Clough in his office. Also there was his then assistant Ron Fenton.

The first thing he said was, 'What are you doing with earrings in, young man?' I told him it was a fashion accessory. He said something in reply — though it wasn't anything untoward. He offered myself and my sister a drink, though I didn't have one myself, then said he had to go. I was awestruck and didn't even ask for an autograph or photo with him — much to my regret in hindsight. I was just caught up in the occasion.

We then went to our seats in the guest box in the Main Stand. At half-time we were allowed to go into the guest area and I saw Brian's older brother and Brian's son Nigel. To my amazement, I also saw Bobby Charlton, Ron Atkinson and Dave Sexton. Brian had given us such a memorable day. Although I never got to meet him again, he gave my sister and I tickets to a few other games.

Meeting Brian was certainly a moment to savour and one I will not forget. I was the envy of my friends at the time — some of whom didn't quite believe that I had sat and had a chat with the great Brian Clough in his office. Brian was down to earth and very friendly and made a lasting impression on me. What a genius he was. Never again will there be anyone like him. RIP, Brian.

Rich Byrne, paramedic: 'I was overwhelmed by the legend.'

I'm a life-long Derby County fan, too young to remember the late Sixties and early Seventies under Clough, but will forever associate him with Derby and indeed Forest's greatest moments. He left us with such a legacy. I had the pleasure of meeting 'Sir' Brian one afternoon while I was working at Derby City Hospital. He stopped to offer a young paramedic his appreciation of my profession. He called me 'son' and was so warm and endearing that I felt overwhelmed. I did, however, manage to stumble the words 'Thank you, Mr Clough.' For me, the man was a true people's man, a legend who drew people to him in both awe and amazement. I'm sad he no longer walks among us, but he will always be with us.

Andrew Thompson, Royal Navy, Plymouth and Derby fan: 'He changed my life.'

I will never forget the day I met Brian Clough – it changed my life. As a young kid living in a Derby children's home, I used to see Brian most Sundays walking his dog in Darley Park. I was always in trouble with the Police and other people, but one day Brian had a little kick around with me, then we sat down and had a chat. His words of wisdom really sank in and changed my life. He was the only person who has had any effect on my life and turned it into a good life instead of going to prison. Thanks for saving me from ruin, Brian Clough. And thanks for making football what it is today, the beautiful game.

Iain Macbriar, QV Associates: 'That special moment when he exchanged thumbs-up signs with my Dad.'

My late father was a lifelong Forest fan (and latterly Cloughie fan), even after we moved to London 45 years ago. We went to the Cup Final and to Nottingham for the parade. We stood on Trent Bridge to watch the team's open-topper go past. My Dad was looking for the Great Man, who was sitting at the back of the top deck. As the bus came alongside, Dad shouted up 'Brian.' The Great Man stood up and looked down over the side of the bus. They made eye contact and exchanged thumbs-up signs. I honestly thought my Dad would have passed away in that moment.

Martin O'Neill, European Cup-winner with Cloughie at Nottingham Forest: 'We often disagreed about my playing ability.'

Brian Clough was uniquely brilliant and so sharp. He knew how to handle the players to get the best out of them. He had everything –

he was an incredible motivator, and he had great awareness. His memory was excellent, and nothing went unnoticed, even in training. He would remember incidents in games that you, as a player, had forgotten about – and you were actually playing in the game!

We would often disagree about my playing ability. I thought I was brilliant – but he didn't. I once went to see him and said I'd like to play in central midfield. He asked me why. We talked for 10 minutes or so, and I thought I was holding my own in the conversation. Then he said to me, 'I'll give you a choice – what number did you play in the last match?' I replied it was number seven. He said: 'Well, what number would you like to play in the next match – number seven or number 12?' Of course, number 12 meant I'd be a substitute. After that, I never bothered him again!

You can never copy someone like Mr Clough and expect to succeed. He was unique. If you copied him, you would end up making mistakes. It's important to be yourself.

It's very difficult to see a provincial club achieving that kind of success again. The big clubs seem to be more established than ever before. But it shouldn't stop you aiming for that kind of success.

(Martin was speaking to the author on stage at the civic reception for the Brian Clough statue in Nottingham.)

Mark Cooling, Lincoln: 'He was simply magnificent.'

My own favourite memory of the great man is from my first game at the City Ground in 1984, when Forest were playing Birmingham City. Only 12 minutes into the match Forest were four goals to nil up, and I could hear someone (distant) screaming. I looked around the stands among the many supporters to try and see who it was.

Finally, I spotted the originator…it was a familiar figure in a green sweatshirt, leaning out of his dugout and giving absolute hell to his defence. I suppose four nil up after just 12 minutes would have been acceptable for other managers. That was him down to a tee…unpredictable, enigmatic and simply magnificent.

On most football shirts, the name on the front of the shirt is more important than the name on the back. For many Forest fans, who wear 'Clough 1' on the back of theirs, it is at least equal.

For so many wonderful, happy and never to be forgotten memories, Brian, I will be grateful for the rest of my life. You are greatly missed, but never forgotten, and your legend will shine brightly as long as the wonderful game of football continues to entertain us all.

Phil Callaway, Elkesley, Nottinghamshire: 'Brian hadn't lost that magic touch.'

I met Brian in London and saw him at his masterful best. As a boy, I supported Forest and had a season ticket up to the age of 18. This was in the late Fifties/early Sixties. After England won the World Cup in 1966 I joined the Army and left the area. Although I occasionally saw Forest when they played in London, the games were few and far between. While I was travelling around the world, Brian joined Forest and I missed the best team in Forest's history.

In the early 1990s I was working and living in London. Brian was doing a book signing at Waterstones in the City, a branch near the Bank of England. I turned up early to get near the front of the queue. It was quite a sight, seeing all the suited bankers waiting to get their books signed by the great man. Brian turned up looking very fit and smartly dressed in a suit, and he got on with the job in hand. He had a word with anyone who cared to ask him anything. I asked when he would next go to a Forest game, and I think he replied that he would go when invited!

After getting my book signed, I was watching proceedings when a very drunk and untidy Geordie swayed into the shop. He was making a lot of noise and being a bit of a nuisance. He swayed up to the desk where Brian was signing and said, 'I went to the same school as you, Brian.' Without batting an eyelid Brian replied, 'Oh yes, which school was that then?' The man named a school, and Brian concurred that he was indeed at that school and went on to persuade the man to leave the shop without any difficulty or fuss. To me, this was an example of his superb man management and personality, bearing in mind he had retired from football. He hadn't lost that magic touch.

Alun Gadd: 'Brian took us by surprise.'

I met him a few times to get his autograph, but one incident always sticks in my mind. When I was a Junior Red all those years ago, about six of us were waiting near the players' entrance before a game one day, when Brian was approaching us. Pens and programmes in hand, we were all wanting his autograph but he just walked straight past us and went inside. I think all of us were thinking what a miserable *!* (or something like that, when you're that young age), but then a few minutes later a steward came out and all of us who had been waiting were told to follow him. He then took us inside and to Brian's office where the great man was sitting behind his desk, and he happily signed our programmes/autograph books etc. Happy or what, as a young kid? It's something I'll never forget about him.

Srikanth Tirupattur, Bangalore, India: 'His influence lives on – even thousands of miles away.'

To me, Brian Clough is one of the most inspirational of figures. From watching him and learning about him, even thousands of miles away in India, I changed the way I thought about things – because of Mr Clough. I went from being almost a melancholic kind of person to someone who was inspired and confident.

I watched the programme on the BBC about his life, it was probably the most absorbing hour of television I have ever seen. I also enjoyed watching the repeat of the Nottingham Forest match when they won the League Championship and Peter Shilton made that incredible save against Coventry that helped win the title. The commentator was talking about that fantastic 42-game unbeaten run. It's not often you can watch a Forest match in India – everybody is crazy about cricket, just like Cloughie was.

Laura J. Zaky: 'RAF Memories.'

My Dad (Harold C. Wolfers) was Brian's football manager in the RAF. He always rated Brian as one of the most talented players. I arranged for Dad and Brian to meet back in the 1980s, and they had a good time. My Dad was so chuffed when Brian brought out his book; it's the only thing he's read from cover to cover in years.

Dave Covey, Thailand: 'Brian's sharp wit.'

When he retired I sent a card thanking him for his contribution to British comedy! Years later he mentioned this in a TV interview, but was unsure whether it was a compliment or an insult. I had the greatest respect for the man, and he made me laugh every time I saw him on TV or in the press.

David Alton, Nottingham: 'The day Brian Clough made my Christmas present complete.'

I planned my encounter with Brian Clough with military precision. I was determined to ask him to sign a book I'd bought as a Christmas present for my young son. The book was John Lawson's *History of Nottingham Forest 1865–1978*. I'd already managed to get all the players to sign it, including Peter Shilton, John Robertson, John McGovern and Kenny Burns. Some of the players from the past had also signed it – names like Jack Burkitt, Terry Hennessey, Bobby McKinlay and Ian Storey Moore. Even the trainer Jimmy Gordon had signed it, as had Peter Taylor.

One of the last names to sign was the author himself, John Lawson. I went to the offices of the *Nottingham Evening Post* and asked at reception if he could sign the book. He kindly came to see me, and after he added his name I told him the only signature I now required was the Great Man – Brian Clough. I told John that I was a bit apprehensive about it, as I had heard Brian could be unpredictable. John said that I should just see how things went on the day – and he advised me to call Brian 'Mr Clough'.

I spent days making sure I'd be in the right place at the right time – assessing what time he usually arrived at the ground, where he parked and where I should stand in order to ask him. On the day I met him, he arrived in his Mercedes and parked outside the reception area, just as I expected. I stood somewhere between the car and the entrance to reception and asked if he'd mind signing the book, which I clutched expectantly. I made sure I called him Mr Clough!

There was no one else waiting, and he invited me inside. I couldn't believe it. I followed him into his office, where he carefully signed the book to my son, with his famous 'Be Good' message. I couldn't thank him enough for making the special Christmas present complete. My son's face on Christmas morning was an absolute picture!

Noel Baldwin, Echuca, Australia: 'Cloughie got me hooked.'

I was never a soccer fan until Cloughie took over Nottingham Forest, and then I was hooked with the success he brought to what was a minnow club. I will never forget the two European Cup triumphs and the accolades they achieved along the way. There will never be another manager like him, a once in a blue moon manager.

Jason Matvijenko: 'A meeting I won't forget.'

I had the pleasure of meeting the great legend, Brian Clough, at Waterstones in Derby, where he was signing copies of his book. I have now got a lovely book with his signature inside – he wrote 'Be Good.' He tried to speak to me, but I told him I am deaf. Still, I won't forget that special day when I met Mr Clough.

Fabrizio Vecchio, Lausanne, Switzerland: 'Simply the best.'

I am Italian, but Cloughie is my idol. He is a fine example of integrity and ability. I consider him to be the best manager ever. I wish there would be someone like him now, but unfortunately the football nowadays is only about money and arrogance. It seems there is no place for people like Cloughie in this world nowadays.

Daniel Horner, Rotherham: 'A special package in the post.'

Many years ago when I was a 'young man' my Mum wrote to all the clubs in the old First Division, hoping to obtain a signed photograph of each team for use as raffle prizes at our annual school fundraiser. Disappointingly, clubs such as Liverpool, Man United and Aston Villa failed to even respond to her polite request. But, lo and behold, a box arrived from none other than the great Brian Clough at Nottingham Forest Football Club, packed with Forest 'goodies'. Now, there were badges, pennants, scarves and programmes etc…lots of wonderful stuff. But curiously no signed team photograph as requested. Sure enough, at the bottom of the box was a huge signed photograph of Brian Clough, with a covering letter which read:

'Dear Mrs Horner – I would be delighted to donate prizes to your school raffle…Please also find enclosed a signed photograph of myself – I would've sent a team photo but the players in my team are far too ugly! Yours, Brian x'

Now that's why Brian Clough is *my* hero!

Selcuk Ozceada, Istanbul, Turkey: 'I met Cloughie in Rome.'

I am a Turkish Cypriot, who emigrated to London at the age of 14.

After meeting my girlfriend at university in London, she went to Nottingham to do her PhD in the fall of 1977. For the next three years I went up to Nottingham every weekend to see her – and that was when I became enchanted by Cloughie.

I was very privileged to go to almost every match at the City Ground in that incredible 1977–78 season, Nottingham Forest's first season in the First Division. The football seemed so simple yet so effective, beating all teams that visited the City Ground. There were unknown players like Woodcock, Withe, Robertson and Anderson – and straight old heads like Shilton, Burns and O'Hare. This was a magical season engulfed in Brian's charm and the only way I can describe it is to say it was like a dream.

To me, the City Ground seemed like a tiny pitch, where my eyes seemed to follow every detail in slow motion. I can still replay them in my head, remembering events like Brian coming out of his dugout and saying 'gentlemen no swearing' to the fans when they were shouting a few swear words to the opposition.

Then it must have been Easter of 1982 when I went abroad for the first time to Rome for a long weekend. On my first night there, I met with a couple of great Syrian lads, who rescued me from the hands of a couple of rogues! The next day we decided to go sightseeing in Rome. I was expecting my Spanish girlfriend to arrive the day after. I was the only one with a camera, so the guys asked if they could put a film in my camera to take some pictures and then they could take the film back to Syria to develop it there, while I could take pictures of the same sights with another film when my girlfriend arrived the next day.

We were walking in front of the Coleseum when God brought me face to face with my greatest idol, Brian Clough, who was also doing a bit of sightseeing, together with his whole Forest team! I could not believe my eyes. Brian was standing three metres in front of me! I was quite shy in those days, but I got together all my courage and went up to Brian and asked him to have a picture taken with me. I was quite scared, not knowing what he would say. He gave me a huge smile, put his arms around my shoulders and said 'Of course we can, my son!' I can't describe the feelings I had at that time and I still remember the moment in the smallest detail. The other guys would not let me have the film, but they promised that they would send it to me in London. They never did.

While I am very upset that that picture was lost to me, I am so grateful that I met Brian and exchanged a few words with him.

May his soul rest in peace. He gave so much pleasure and inspiration to so many people and certainly has been an important part of my life.

Mark Pitt, Atlanta, United States: 'Brian was pure magic.'

I only saw you once Bri – you were in your famous green sweatshirt alongside Peter, and I was a young kid in the stands at Coventry's Highfield Road ground.

Although I was a mad Coventry City supporter, you and your team were the example of the 'magic' of football. Your genius was not lost on this young kid, and I will always remember the 'Yarwood, follow that' line on the *Whole World in Our Hands* record – what superb comedy that was.

Keith Landles, Edinburgh: 'He was simply magnificent.'

I'm Scottish and I'm 54 years of age. I never met Mr Clough, but I feel like I grew up with him. He was always on the telly and seemed like a family friend, being in our living room so often, as a regular visitor to my home. One of my favourite stories about Brian is how – on travelling on the team coach to Celtic Park, from Glasgow Airport – he spotted the pub run by the then Celtic manager Davie Hay and ordered the bus to stop and all his staff off and into the pub, to enjoy some 'refreshment.' Players, trainers, etc all had a drink – at the expense of Davie Hay as, when Clough was asked to settle the bar bill, he referred the barman to see 'the Celtic manager!' Nottingham Forest had their 'away goal' safely tucked away after that bit of psychology. Brilliant stuff from one of the true originals, and there weren't many, even then!

Colin Shields, Nottingham: 'My Malta memory.'

When Brian was managing Forest, we were all invited to Malta as guests of the Maltese Government. They put on special receptions and presentations for us. They even took us out to the island of Gozo on one of their naval ships. The captain heard that I had been in the Navy and even allowed me to steer the ship. I turned to Brian and said: 'This is fabulous, isn't it?' 'Fabulous?' he replied, 'I can't wait to get off this ship fast enough – I hate ships!'

We got to Gozo and signed the special visitors book – on the page was the signature of the Queen and Prince Philip, from a previous visit, and below that was 'Nottingham Forest' and my name.

Then they played the inaugural game at a stadium in Malta's capital, Valletta. When we arrived at the stadium we sat in the directors' box. Brian said: 'Col, you come and sit with me.' So, there we are, sitting in the box – with the President of Malta sitting directly in front of us. But on the way to the stadium we'd seen a lot of protests and people with placards – there was quite a lot of civil unrest that day. I turned to Brian and said: 'I'm not happy sitting just here.' He replied: 'Why? What's the matter with you?' I told him: 'If anyone decides to assassinate the President, and they miss, they're going to hit either you or me.' Brian replied: 'Hey, you're spot on. Come on, let's move.' So we did – and we left unscathed.

Peter Shilton, European Cup-winner (twice) with Cloughie at Nottingham Forest: 'I think we had a lot of things in common.'
Brian Clough was like nobody else. He was very dynamic – that's the thing that impressed me when I first met him. He had a tremendous personality. He could be tough, but he could also be very understanding and I think you need that in order to be a successful manager.

I got on with him particularly well. I think we had a lot of things in common. But the one big thing was that you could always trust him to be honest. He always treated everybody the same – it didn't matter whether you were one of the star players in the club or whether you were the tea-lady, everybody was treated the same.

Mark Faulkner, BBC journalist: 'The day I was nearly run over by Cloughie.'

Growing up in the Allestree area of Derby, sightings of Brian Clough were common and always recounted. But I'd never seen him. Yet when it came, my encounter with him turned out to be a little more fraught than I expected. Aged around nine or 10, I walked across the bottom of Woodlands Road without looking where I was going. There was a screech of tyres and I looked round in horror. Sure enough, there was the familiar red t-shirt and that famous green jumper leaning out of the car window. A stern 'Young man, watch how you go!' followed. I apologised and scuttled off, proud to say I'd almost been run over by Old Big 'Ead. It's safe to say that from that day on I always remember my version of the Green Clough Code!

Amanda Tongue, Nottingham: 'The day I nearly ran over Brian Clough.'

It started like any ordinary morning, but turned into the day I almost knocked over a football legend. I was driving in the West Bridgford area of Nottingham, near the newsagents run by Brian's son, Simon. The traffic was going quite slowly, in fact the line of cars eventually came to a standstill. The queue was about to pick-up speed again when I noticed a figure step off the pavement at the last moment. It seemed a bit unusual as there was an official pedestrian crossing a little further up the road. Before I could put my foot on the accelerator any further I quickly braked to make sure I didn't hit the man who had stepped out. Then I realised who it was. Brian Clough turned towards me and gave his famous thumbs-up signal before blowing me a kiss. I just sat there for a moment, mesmerised. A kiss from my football hero — you can't beat that!

Mike Carey, BBC Radio Derby broadcaster and former newspaper journalist: 'I was staggered when he took me inside the football stadium and introduced me as a member of Derby's training staff!'

Many years ago, as an aspiring young sports writer on the *Derby Evening Telegraph*, I summoned the nerve to ask Harry Storer, the Derby County manager (who famously did not suffer fools gladly) his opinion of a Middlesbrough forward line which had just administered a 7–1 defeat to his side on their own Baseball Ground. 'Four cowards and Clough!' came the somewhat contemptuous retort. Little did any of us dream that the self-same Brian Clough would one day return to Derby and not only revitalise an ailing football club beyond recognition, but influence many lives, mine included.

Let it be said at once that the Clough I knew (and hugely respected) bore no resemblance to the gross caricature of the man that appeared in a recent book and film. Unlike many a less-talented manager of his era, he was approachable, humorous, generous and – not many people will know this – perhaps more insecure than you might think. Thus, he was not keen on going anywhere by himself, which is why one day I found myself accompanying him in his blue Rover to a London football ground to inquire about a player.

I was staggered when he took me inside the stadium with him and introduced me to the manager as a member of Derby's training staff! The home manager eyed me somewhat quizzically, but the episode passed without comment and there was no transfer deal. On the return journey, though, I did have to wait in the car outside Filbert Street while Brian went inside to talk to Leicester City's manager Matt Gillies, a visit which like the earlier one was completely unannounced. As we completed our trip up the M1, Brian casually revealed that he had just attempted to buy Peter Shilton...a deal he did not achieve until some years later.

That episode perhaps offered a clue about Clough's driving ambition, and as his son Nigel struggles to introduce quality to the current Rams side he must envy the freedom with which his father operated. For instance, after paying a record fee for Sunderland's Colin Todd, he announced to the assembled Press, with tongue only slightly in cheek: 'We've just signed the best ball-winner in British football – I think I'd better tell the chairman!'

Some time later I became Brian's amanuensis, writing his twice-weekly column for a national newspaper. Between times he would discuss his plans for the future. 'Eventually we will have a team here so good that even you could manage it,' he would say. 'Every year we will just go out and buy just one player – but he will be the best player in the country.'

Sadly, for Derby County, that theory was never put to the test. It was a privilege to work with Brian Clough. Most of the time, it was a question of what to leave out of his column, not what to put in (unlike the case of another well-known manager who expected his ghost writer to have his column written *before* they met up each week!). I'll never forget the morning when he burst into his office and said enthusiastically: 'I've got today's intro – what a week it's been for saying "bugger me!"'

I get the feeling Brian Clough would have found many weeks like that today. He would have had much to say about football agents, about managers who criticise referees or who can't control their players and even – or may be especially – about England managers who can't speak English. And – young man – it would have all made sense.

Mick Somers, one of Cloughie's first signings at Hartlepool: 'He made sure I received the best care that money could buy.'

Cloughie would sometimes take us training on the beach at Seaton Carew, not far from Hartlepool. I remember we were on our way there one day when he saw an old lady struggling to cross the road. Without hesitation, he got our minibus to stop so he could get out and help her. He walked her across the road and then gave her a 10-bob note. That was the kind of man he was.

I got on like a house on fire with Cloughie; he was a lovely bloke. He had that magic quality to get the best out of his players. If you did the business on the pitch, that's where it mattered. I admired his straight-talking. He was so honest with you and I appreciated that. If you had a bad game, he'd tell you. Cloughie was a fantastic goalscorer and you were in awe of him all the time, because you were playing for one of the all-time great goalscorers.

I enjoyed playing for him, but if you stepped out of line you'd be in trouble. Even as a young man of 33 or 34, he was a disciplinarian. At Hartlepool I lived in digs with four other players, and one of them was a lad who didn't always tow the line and used to like a drink. But Cloughie knew everything that went on, and he came up with a great way of stopping this lad from going out the night before matches. He'd come round to our house and say 'Come with me, young man', and he'd get him to spend the night babysitting for his children!

I joined Hartlepool from Torquay. To this day, I still remember the Torquay chairman telling me that he'd had an approach from Hartlepool, who were obviously interested in signing me. Clough and his assistant Peter Taylor had just taken over there and were willing to pay three or four thousand pounds to sign me. It was February and I told them I'd probably be able to leave on a free transfer at the end of the season, so why not wait til then? They agreed – so we shook hands on the deal in February, for us to get in contact when the season was over.

In the meantime, I received a few more offers from other clubs and I had nothing confirmed from Hartlepool, just a verbal agreement. Then I received a phone call from Cloughie. 'Why haven't I heard from you?' he asked. 'Are you going somewhere else?'

'To be honest, Brian, I thought you would have phoned me,' I replied. I explained that I still wanted to join Hartlepool – and what swung the deal for me was that a few other Nottinghamshire lads were interested in joining too. So we all met Brian at the White Post Hotel in Nottinghamshire and agreed terms and signed-up there and then.

Brian became like a father figure to me. I feel very privileged to have played for him. He really was something else. Even though he was new to management when I knew him, you could tell he had something special, and it was obvious that Hartlepool was just a small stepping stone for him onto bigger things. He was destined to be one of the best football managers who ever lived.

Hartlepool were a team that always used to finish in the bottom four of the old Fourth Division, but when Cloughie came in he turned the club around. By the end of his second season at the club, we'd finished in the top half of the League.

I played about 25 games and then I had a knee injury – I did it against Notts County at Meadow Lane. It was so bad that I needed a cartilage operation. Cloughie sent me to see the same specialist he'd had at Sunderland, when he suffered the injury which finished his playing career. They looked after me really well.

On two or three occasions Cloughie took me up to Sunderland in his car. He made sure I had the best care – the best that money could buy, although my injury was nowhere near as bad as his had been.

I still have a newspaper cutting from November 1968 when Hartlepool were facing Shrewsbury in the FA Cup. Cloughie is quoted as saying: 'It really is disappointing that the injury has come at a time like this – possibly when we needed Mick's qualities more than at any time.'

Clough and Taylor eventually left to take over at Derby. But they'd laid some strong foundations, because the following season we actually gained promotion to the old Third Division for the first time in the club's history.

I played a few matches in the Third Division but then realised I couldn't continue, after going back to see the specialist at

Sunderland. The knee injury ended my career. I was granted a testimonial at Hartlepool, and so I went to see Cloughie at Derby's Baseball Ground to ask if he'd bring his side up to the North East for the game. He knew what had happened to me, and his reply was immediate: 'Of course I will.'

On the day of the match, Brian asked me to make sure that one particular Hartlepool player didn't kick one of his players – so I went into the dressing room and passed on the message. Cloughie did me proud that day, he didn't even ask for expenses to cover the team's travel costs. That's the way the man was. He was so generous.

Duncan McKenzie, who signed for Cloughie at Leeds United: 'My Charity Shield request.'

Quite simply, Brian Clough was the greatest manager ever. He broke the mould and was Box Office wherever he went. I'll always be grateful for everything he did for me. I remember before the Charity Shield match at Wembley, I asked him for two complementary tickets for my parents. He replied: 'If your mother and father won't pay to see you play, how can you expect anyone else to?'

(Duncan was the special guest speaker at the Gala Dinner held in the Ballroom of Nottingham's Council House in June 2006, to raise money for Nottingham's bronze statue of Brian Clough.)

Brendan Hunt, a Nottinghamshire police officer: 'I was on duty at Brian's last home League match – and came face to face with him on the pitch.'

I'll never forget that day. Funnily enough, I wasn't a football fan at the time, and that day I had no idea that it was Brian's last match. It didn't dawn on me, until I saw the footage many times on telly, on the internet and in the papers, what a really momentous day it was. I was on duty in one of the stands and remember the fans going onto the pitch to surround Brian.

I recall pushing through the crowd, who were making towards Brian, and with two or three other officers formed a Police cordon around him, to offer him some protection from the crowd who were simply mobbing him. He looked tired and almost beaten, and perhaps a little overwhelmed. I said to him, 'Are you alright Brian?' and he replied, 'Oh yes, young man!' and he continued to conduct his pitch farewell. I don't really remember how Brian escaped the pitch invasion around him, or really what happened next, but this pitch walk seemed a long and exhausting one.

I try to get to the City Ground as often as I can, and the events of that day come back to me each time I go. I mainly sit in the Brian Clough Stand and try to recall which set of stairs I was standing on when the pitch was invaded, but I can't. I can just remember whereabouts I was on the pitch when I came face to face with Brian Clough, and an event I shall never forget.

Jon Phipps, Bristol: 'I won't forget what a firm handshake he had!'
I drove 120 miles to make sure I met Brian Clough. I'd read on the tribute website, brianclough.com, that he was appearing in Burton-on-Trent for a signing session for his book *Walking on Water*. So I set-off at 7am from my home in Bristol to make the 240-mile round trip by car with my friend George.

We were there so early I think he thought we were from the Press! But he couldn't have been nicer to us and it was an absolute honour to meet him. A big crowd built-up behind us. I was really pleased that I went there because he died just over a year later.

I'd always been interested in Brian Clough, even though I don't support any of the clubs he was associated with. He was the last of the great managers. He took two clubs from the lower reaches of the Second Division and turned them into champions. His man-management was fantastic.

The day I met him is something I will always remember. And I'll never forget what a firm handshake he had! I had a photograph taken with him and it's now proudly on my desk.

David Howlett: 'An e-mail to Brian from January 2003.'

I met you once – inside the entrance to the main office at Forest. I tried to get a ticket for the League Cup Final against Southampton, as my mate had forgotten to go on the correct day with my season ticket. I was told in the local social club to try the Forest secretary's office, but I thought they said his name was Mr Wright. So off I went and you asked me where I was going. You were with Peter Taylor and Peter Shilton. Your reply was 'His name's White, get it right!' which seemed to amuse you at the time. But you opened the ticket office early for me when you saw me queuing two hours later. I've never forgotten that.

Chris Meakin: 'An e-mail to Brian from February 2003.'

I was fortunate to be watching my beloved Forest for a year or so before you arrived. What happened after that was absolute dreamland, *Roy of the Rovers* stuff and some of the happiest times of my life. I have been a season ticket holder right up to the present day.

Never before have I felt the urge to speak to anyone famous or in the public eye, as I am not easily impressed by that sort of thing. After the County Cup Final I just couldn't help myself and waited for nearly three hours behind the Main Stand to see you.

Eventually Archie Gemmill brought me in to see your good self and you gave me a few moments of your precious time and signed a picture for me, which still stands proudly in my office at home. Thank you for such amazing memories over the years.

Brian Berger: 'An e-mail to Brian from March 2003.'

It was really good, at last, to be able to meet you in person at the Burton game on Saturday 22 March. I was born in Farnborough on 21 March 1946, so we share the same birthday. I have always been a great admirer of yours, as has my son, Richard, who for his sins is still a supporter of Nottingham Forest! You have a lot to answer for!

I enjoy the atmosphere and involvement of non-League football, and here at Farnborough Town Football Club we have had our full share of events in recent months. The highlight of the season, though, has been the FA Cup match at Highbury against Arsenal, and I am sure that you will appreciate how much these games mean to clubs like Burton and Farnborough.

May I wish you a full recovery and that you live a long and happy life. As I said to you on Saturday, I had a Subarachnoid Haemorrhage and a stroke last August and that with the determination that us guys have, have made a near full recovery. Meeting you on Saturday made all the effort worthwhile.

Chris Harrison, Manchester United fan: 'An e-mail from September 2004.'

Thanks for the memories Brian and for the colour you brought to all our lives. I would have loved you to have come to Old Trafford in your pomp, what a thought!

As a 44-year-old, I remember the great days of black-and-white TV (*Match Of The Day*) and white pitches with orange balls in the winter. I also remember a manager in a green top who sent out his teams to play the game the 'right way' and to respect the rule of law without dissent. I also remember a working class hero who never forgot his roots and remained loyal to 'his' people all his life and never sold out.

I studied in the East Midlands for a couple of years and I became friends with both Derby and Forest fans, and I know the feelings they both had for Cloughie. This feeling, however, was not just shared by fans of Derby and Forest, Brian left his mark on all of us and in our own way we also feel your grief at his loss.

RIP Cloughie and thanks for the memories – we all died a little the day you left us!

Paul Hubbard, Torrevieja, Spain: 'A trip to the barbers – by order of the boss.'

I met Mr Clough when I was a young player at Brighton in the Seventies. He told me to get a haircut or I'd never be a footballer. I was at the barbers that afternoon. When he spoke, people listened, because he talked sense.

Richard Childs, artist: 'He told me I'd made him look attractive!'

I met Brian on the last home match of the season on the day he retired…it's still a great memory.

Basically, I'd been given the contract for completing artwork of the Forest team through the commercial shop, and Brian had seen one of the pictures of him with the team. He then instructed the chairman Fred Reacher to arrange a meeting with us before kick-off so that the Gedling Supporters Club could present him with the picture.

Myself, my wife and Joan Bakewell of the branch parked in the Forest car park and were led through 30 or so paparazzi to meet the chairman as planned. There were so many photographers there because it was Cloughie's last day in management. We arrived in Fred's office, which was amazing – waiting for our idol. Eventually, Fred and Cloughie came in and met us.

We introduced ourselves, and he gave all the girls a big hug, it was an emotional scene. When he came to me as I clutched my artwork, I went to shake his hand and he said, 'You're not getting away with that young man, give us a hug!' There I was, hugging the legend on the most important day in Forest's history. I was blown away. When I presented him with the painting, he said, 'My word young man, you've made me look pretty.' I said it was a bit of artistic licence, and he laughed and called me cheeky.

Anyway, we had coffee and talked about the future for him and the Reds. It was surreal. Half an hour later I sat down in my usual Trent End seat with minutes to spare before kick-off. The guy at the side of me thought I wasn't coming as I always got there well before kick-off. I told him that I'd just been hugging Cloughie and talking football. He just looked at me and thought I was pulling his leg. I said that I wasn't lying, and he just changed the subject. What a day!

Also, a year earlier I had my wedding photos taken on the pitch and I received a signed wedding card from Brian and Barbara Clough. When we left a couple of weeks later to start a new life in Australia we received a good luck card too. Months later, when it was our anniversary, we then got cards from the Cloughs and Psycho. That showed why Cloughie was the people's football genius. He cared for his supporters, wherever they were.

John Quinn, New York, United States: 'The man who attracted me to soccer – even all these miles away.'

I'm a 49-year-old sports fanatic from Brooklyn. My first loves are baseball and American football, but soccer (or just football as it's called in the UK) came into my life on an ordinary day in 1977. And Brian Clough was a big part of it.

The local PBS station broadcast a soccer show called 'All-Star Soccer' every Saturday afternoon in the USA and Canada. It was a match from England, usually from the First Division, that was played the previous weekend, and the show was edited down to 60 minutes. I watched it one day almost by accident, and I was hooked. I wanted to know more about the English game the more I watched. And this was the year that Nottingham Forest were promoted to the First Division after spending a number of years in the Second Division. I remember watching great players like Peter Shilton, Martin O'Neill, Archie Gemmill and John Robertson. Forest jumped out to a great start that year, so many of their matches were broadcast that season.

And I'll never forget when announcer Mario Machado would tell stories of Forest's colorful manager, Brian Clough. He would tell the audience about his days as Derby County's manager and leading them out of the Second Division to the top tier and then to an English League Championship in 1972, and also about his very short but eventful stint with Leeds United. I'll never forget hearing the stories of his players' loyalty to him, like John O'Hare and John McGovern, who played for him at both Derby and Leeds, and followed him to Nottingham Forest.

I instantly became a Nottingham Forest fan, and Brian Clough was a big part in me becoming not just a Forest fan but an English football fan. It was great to see Forest win the title in that first year back, and then two European Championships. I am still a fan to this day, watching matches here in America on the Fox Soccer Channel.

And I thank Brian Clough for my soccer fandom. You were the greatest manager the English national team never had. And I thank you so much for showing this American what a beautiful game soccer is when it is played right. I must admit I pull for Liverpool, but I always keep an eye on how Forest are doing and I'm rooting for them to return to the Premiership.

I'm sure that would make Mr Clough very happy, wherever he is.

Peter Smith, London: 'As a teenager on trial at the City Ground, I had to call him Mr Clough.'

I would just like to extend my gratitude to you for finding time and the will to honour a legend like Mr Clough. I call him this because when I arrived at the City Ground for a trial aged 14 he insisted I address him so – whereas my uncle Eddie was permitted to call him Brian.

Although I was only at your great club a short while, the man left his mark on me and I will never forget him. I have just recently got my coaching qualifications, and it is principally down to Mr Clough's inspiration that I chose to go down this route.

It is shameful that English football as a whole doesn't give him his full credit, but there are those of us who realise that some people are too important to be forgotten. I must point out at this juncture that I am a lifelong Liverpool fan and a proud Dubliner – but his effect on my life and my football thinking is a testimony to the power of this one-off human being.

Marco Baguley, New Zealand: 'That European Cup parade.'
Brian Clough was and always will be my hero. My fondest memories are of Brian and the team showing off the European Cup in the Old Market Square in Nottingham and Brian signing my Forest shirt. Still have the shirt. Long live Brian's memories.

Chris Plant, Hull City fan: 'I was mesmerised by Cloughie.'
My own father was a football manager for about 20 years, so I can relate to Nigel Clough in a way. I first came across 'Old Big 'Ead' when I was watching TV at the age of about six. I was watching my own father get ready for another match on a cold Sunday afternoon in Hull. For some reason I was mesmerised by Cloughie that day.

Although I'm Hull City through and through, I did have a weak spot for Nottingham Forest when Brian Clough was in charge. The reason I loved Cloughie was because he said what he thought (right or wrong). I like people like that; I know where I stand with them. Cloughie was a sharp man, a very quick thinker and always had an answer ready.

God bless Brian Clough, you had a way with words – and I love you 'Old Big 'Ead'.

Paul Ellis, former chairman of the Nottingham Forest Supporters' Club and the Brian Clough Statue Fund (Nottingham): 'A day to be remembered.'

When I began watching Nottingham Forest in 1958, I could never have dreamed that they would achieve the level of success that Brian Clough brought to the City Ground. His arrival was like a whirlwind, and he conjured up some magical times which Forest fans will never forget. But it wasn't only about the trophies. The type of football his teams played was entertaining to watch and his players were told to respect the officials – unlike many of today's professionals. His achievements won the admiration of fans around the globe.

I was proud to become chairman of the small committee which raised funds for Nottingham's Brian Clough statue. We smashed through the £60,000 fund-raising target within just 18 months. The way that fans contributed to the project was a clear indication of how much affection they still have for a remarkable man. The unveiling of the statue was a very proud day for everyone involved and – although I wasn't fortunate to meet Brian during his time at the City Ground – I was honoured to present Mrs Clough with a bouquet of flowers at a private event after the unveiling. It was certainly a day to be remembered.

Graham Wilde, MM Canada Ltd, Canada: 'My tribute – from a Man United fan.'

The best tribute I can pay Brian is that I witnessed his Nottingham Forest champions-elect come to Old Trafford on 17 December 1977 and destroy Manchester United 4–0 in front of 54,000 people. I've seen teams win well at Old Trafford before, but no team has outclassed United so spectacularly in my time as a Reds fan. It was a pleasure to witness a team come and perform like that, even if the team I was supporting was on the receiving end.

Brian was a complete one-off in terms of achievement, character and status. Of course, there have been other successful characters like him, but none are loved and remembered as fondly as he is today. He is sorely missed as a person, and particularly in football.

Malcolm Cook, Spurs fan: 'I saw him play for Sunderland.'

I consider myself extremely lucky as I got to see Cloughie play during his time at Sunderland. Over the years I have seen some of the greatest players, but the greatest three for me were John Charles, Len Shackleton and, of course, Brian Clough. Due to the blazer brigade at the FA we will never know what heights England may have achieved under the managerial skills of the late and great Brian Clough, but I'd lay a pound to a penny that we would have achieved far more than we have to date…and that's from a Spurs fan!

Steve Colman, Dubai: 'My special memory of Cloughie's Sunderland visit.'

I was doing the PA at Sunderland's Stadium of Light when Cloughie came onto the pitch. A colleague interviewed the Great Man pitchside. I was dead jealous until he asked Cloughie what he thought of the new stadium. Quick as a flash, in front of 42,000 people, the Great One spoke 'Young man, it's far better looking than you.' My pal dissolved as the crowd lapped it up. I'm now working in Dubai and want to thank you for keeping me in touch with the reality of life, namely Football.

Garry Roberts, Christchurch, New Zealand: 'It was fascinating to read about Brian – on the other side of the world.'

Back in the halcyon days of the Sixties and Seventies the information we received here in New Zealand was a lot less efficient than it obviously is today. In fact, if you were a young man (excuse the pun) you basically had to rely on Brian Moore's *Match of the Day* replayed on a Sunday lunchtime – and the very good *Shoot* magazine. Those were in the days when *Shoot* was published in a newsprint form rather than the glossy magazines that are printed today.

In those days, the magazine was full of information and you could always read something either about Derby or Brian Clough in its pages. Brian Clough hogged the headlines, as he rightly deserved, and brought with him a style that was a whiff of fresh air from what had preceded him. In some ways, what the tribute website, brianclough.com, is doing is what the foundations for the likes of Elvis and Marilyn Munroe are doing. Keeping the memory alive and passing down its legacy. Good for you.

Jamie Blake, Nottingham: 'My ever-lasting memory of meeting Brian.'

It was the summer of 2004 and my nine-year-old son JJ and I were walking down Central Avenue in West Bridgford. We walked into the news shop which is managed by Simon Clough and his family to buy a newspaper. I noticed out of the corner of my eye a very frail but instantly recognisable Brian Clough sitting on a stool just to the left of the counter.

I asked him how he was and told him what an honour it was to meet him again, as it had been 30 years since I had been in his presence. He asked me where that had been and I explained that I had been a 13-year-old Leeds United schoolboy in 1974 when he had taken over the managerial reigns there. He responded jokingly, shouting 'Don't hit me, don't hit me!'

I, also jokingly, reassured him that I wouldn't and then told him what I thought of him: that he was, in my opinion, the greatest club manager there had ever been and that had Peter Taylor joined him at Leeds – and in turn they had been given the time – then the 'glory years' that Forest enjoyed would have been in Yorkshire instead.

He then turned the conversation on to me and my son, asking us where we lived and what we did. JJ responded by explaining that he was a Nottingham Forest Academy player. Brian made such a fuss of him and told him to keep working hard, and he would play for Forest's first team in time.

JJ has been offered a professional playing contract with Nottingham Forest on his 17th birthday, and he now fully understands who the great Brian Clough was.

Brian Clough died seven days after our meeting.

Neil Blake, Nottingham: 'I hung the first scarf in tribute to Cloughie.'

As grey, over-cast September Mondays go, nothing prepared us for what was about to be announced on the TV. I was off work for a day, a rest day for a tram driver, when rumours were posted on a Forest chat forum that Brian Clough had died. My initial thought, because of who posted the comment, was to dismiss it as a sick rumour.

Then another was posted…then another. I walked into the living room, put on Sky Sports News…and saw it for myself. One snapshot, a grey photo of Brian Clough, with the headline 'Brian Clough 1935–2004'.

Never again will we hear him on the radio. Never again will we read his thoughts in the newspapers. Never again will we see that familiar twinkle in his eyes, on the TV. He'd fought all he could but, unlike most things he came across, the cancer had beaten him.

I phoned my Dad, who was at work. I choked on my words when I broke the news to him. A strange reaction to someone who I wasn't related to – and had never actually met. But he was part of my life for as long as I remember. I was born in 1974 and Brian Clough played a massive part in my childhood.

My Dad was stunned. The day seemed even greyer.

The next part of my day seems odd even now. I don't know why, but I wanted to go to the ground. Is this what people do when heroes die? What was procedure? Where, in the fan's manual, does it tell you what to do?

I put on a Forest jacket and bombed, if you can possibly bomb on a Vespa, to the City Ground.

Once I got there, I was met by a variety of reporters and a few security guards in their hi-vis jackets. I parked my bike at the front gate and walked around the car park. One reporter asked me for a comment. Feeling awkward, I declined.

The day was getting greyer and windier by the minute. After a short while I asked the security guard if I could tie my scarf to the main gates. He said I could and I did so. A few moments later another passer by hanged a Villa scarf next to mine.

If there were no more scarves to be added to the gate, this alone would have shown the widespread recognition of the man.

A member of the press was then pestering the security guard. He informed the hack that I was the first to hang up my scarf, so ushered him in my direction. This happened a few times.

During this time, a few more people were hanging up their scarves. They were scarves which had seen many a fine victory both home and away, but were to be retired in honour of the man who led us to those victories.

A short while later, a security guard removed the scarves, to lay them in front of the old ticket office windows in the Main Stand car park. The wind picked up and they blew all over the place. The same guard attempted to tie them to a nearby traffic cone.

Is this all we could do to honour the man who led us to two European Cup successes? A few of the small crowd that had now joined us in the car park were showing their dissent towards this idea and the scarves were then moved to the gate at the end of the building and near the wall of the players' car park…where the floral tributes were to be eventually laid.

Kenny Burns and Roger Davies, who at the time had a local radio phone-in show, came and went, expressing their condolences. Brian's former secretary, Carole Washington, barely 5ft in height but an absolute Forest giant, was movingly distraught. Being from Carlton, I'd spoken to Carole a few times, when I worked behind a local bar, and she always told me great Cloughie stories. She was even kind enough to get his autobiography signed for me.

'To Neil, Be Good, Best Wishes Brian Clough x x x' One of the very few treasured material goods I own.

The afternoon went on, the fans came down, the cameras clicked and the journalists relayed copy. Nottingham was greyer than it had been for years.

I stayed for a few hours. Saw a few familiar faces. Reminisced about the glory days and shared BC stories. By now the offices were closing and people were starting to come down in larger numbers.

I decided to leave. Somewhat heavier hearted than when I woke up that September morning.

The day my hero died.

Pat Brett, born in the Meadows, Nottingham, now living in West Virginia, United States: 'A special memory.'

One afternoon I was sitting on the banks of the River Trent. Along the path beside the river came BC – green sweatshirt, white shorts, white socks and trainers, hands behind his back, obviously thinking about the game that evening. I waved, he waved back. 'Good luck tonight, I'll be there,' I said. 'We'll try to win for you,' he said. Of course, we did.

David Prowse – whose poem in tribute to Cloughie was recited by Barbara Clough at the memorial service at Pride Park in October 2004.

I very much admired what Brian Clough achieved during his career and it inspired me to write this poem. His achievements were really remarkable. When you think he got injured at just 29 and then went into management and became so successful at it. It was very gratifying for me when Barbara Clough read the poem at the memorial service. It was nice to know that my own personal tribute was part of that special occasion.

'Cloughie'

What made him so endearing is elusive to explain,

This tyrant in a sweatshirt barking orders in the rain.

Today he offered vitriol, tomorrow marzipan,

A paradox, a puzzle but a diamond of a man.

When the Gods apportioned modesty, one youngster wasn't there,

He was in the queue marked confidence, receiving twice his share.

With two good feet beneath him he considered it enough,

And so was born the character we know as Brian Clough.

Young Cloughie did things his way, for no one showed him how,

Emerging from the backstreets like a blossom on a bow.

Becoming proud and peerless as a hero of his time,

And then, one tackle later, down and out at twenty-nine.

Where others might have wilted or nestled in their grief,

Cloughie found salvation in his cocky self belief.

Come set-back or adversity, a man is still a man,

So it was, as one dream ended, that another one began.

Reality was Hartlepool, the lowest of them all,

In the Fourth Division basement with their backs against the wall.

All patchwork roofs and puddles and frostbite in the shade,

It was hard and it was humbling, but the boy would learn his trade.

Along came Peter Taylor and the dugout was complete,

Two canny minds would meet and merge to share the judgement seat.

Two mop and bucket soldiers to pound a broken drum,

But the cavalry would gather and the glory days would come.

For Cloughie had a quality no training could provide,

The gift of lending common men the jauntiness of stride.

Players tapped abilities they didn't know were there,

And good ones climbed to greatness on a goading and a glare.

Cloughie's team played football in the manner meant to be,

A joy for those who wore his shirt and those who came to see,

No arguments, no ego trips, no stars to shine alone,

As Cloughie scolded, Cloughie scowled, and loved them as his own.

For behind the bullish phrases, all the arrogance and pride,

There beat a kindly human heart, as deep as it was wide.

Deserving of an epitaph, significant but sad,

Just the greatest England manager that England never had.

The Last Word – Richard Hallam, Nottingham.

Back in December 2008 I was lucky enough to attend the Civic Reception to celebrate the wonderful bronze statue of Brian Clough in Nottingham. The event was held at the Council House, following the highly successful unveiling of the sculpture the previous month, when 5,000 fans came to see their hero immortalised in bronze. The guests of honour at that special evening in the Council House Ballroom were Mr Clough's family.

It was an unforgettable evening – and for me, there was an extra-special memory. It was the moment when the superb sculpture had three special visitors on that cold winter's night.

European Cup heroes Martin O'Neill, John Robertson and Garry Birtles had been special guests at the Civic Reception. Martin and John had been unable to attend the unveiling in person because of their European commitments at the time with Aston Villa. So after the reception, they all walked the short distance to see the sculpture. It was the first time Martin and 'Robbo' had seen the statue, close-up, for themselves.

I spotted them looking up at their Gaffer, as he stood there bathed in the spotlights. For a few precious minutes they were united again – Old Big 'Ead and his young men. I imagine they reminisced a little about the good old days and those glorious achievements, unlikely to be seen again. As the three European Cup legends stood in front of the 9ft-high statue, I reckon the Master Manager also had a few comments for them. 'Hey, young men,' he might have said. 'You always thought I was larger than life – now here's the proof, and in bronze too!' Trust Cloughie to have the last word.

If you would like to share a memory of meeting Brian Clough,

e-mail Marcus Alton at youngman@brianclough.com

ND - #0287 - 270225 - C0 - 210/136/13 - PB - 9781908234988 - Matt Lamination